State Health Insurance Market Reform

Since the late 1980s many US states have sought to incrementally reform their health insurance markets. The intent of such reform has been quite straightforward: to ensure access to affordable health insurance by addressing insurer practices perceived to be exclusionary. In the light of this, a compelling public policy issue is whether these efforts to address disparities in the population's access to health insurance have been successful or have yielded unintended consequences.

This volume provides a critical assessment of the current state of knowledge on insurance market reform that is accessible to both policymakers and researchers. The contributions provide a critical evaluation of empirical research findings, applied methodologies, and policy implications associated with state reform of small-group and individual insurance markets.

With contributions from internationally respected health economists, as well as industry, regulatory, and consumer representatives, this book will prove to be a useful read for all those with an interest in the economics of healthcare.

Alan C. Monheit is Professor of Health Economics in the Department of Health Systems and Policy, School of Public Health, at the University of Medicine and Dentistry of New Jersey, USA. **Joel C. Cantor** is Director of the Center for State Health Policy and Professor of Public Policy at Rutgers, the State University of New Jersey, USA.

Routledge international studies in health economics

Edited by Charles Normand

London School of Hygiene and Tropical Medicine

and

Richard M. Scheffler

School of Public Health, University of California

State Health Insurance Market Reform

Toward inclusive and sustainable health insurance markets

Edited by Alan C. Monheit and Joel C. Cantor

Routledge
Taylor & Francis Group
LONDON AND NEW YORK

First published 2004
by Routledge
2 Park Square, Milton Park, Abingdon, Oxfordshire OX14 4RN

Simultaneously published in the USA and Canada
by Routledge
711 Third Ave, New York, NY 10017

Routledge is an imprint of the Taylor & Francis Group

Typeset in Times by Wearset Ltd, Boldon, Tyne and Wear

British Library Cataloguing in Publication Data
A catalogue record for this book is available from the British Library

Library of Congress Cataloging in Publication Data
A catalog record for this book has been requested

ISBN 0-415-70035-3

To our families

Contents

Figures

Tables

Contributors

Thomas C. Buchmueller, Ph.D., is an Associate Professor of Health Care at the University of California, Irvine, Graduate School of Business. He earned his Ph.D. at the University of Wisconsin, Madison. His primary areas of research are health economics, particularly the economics of employer-provided health insurance, health insurance reform and managed competition. Professor Buchmueller's publications include articles in the *Journal of Health Economics*, *Journal of Human Resources*, *Industrial and Labor Relations Review*, *Health Economics*, *Health Affairs and Inquiry*. He is a Faculty Associate of UCI's Research Unit in Health Policy and Research and a Faculty Research Fellow of the National Bureau of Economic Research.

Deborah J. Chollet, Ph.D., is a Senior Fellow with the Research Division of Mathematica Policy Research, in Washington, DC. In this position, she is responsible for leading research projects related to health insurance coverage, markets, and financing. Dr. Chollet received her Ph.D. in economics from the Maxwell School of Citizenship and Public Affairs at Syracuse University and was previously a Vice-President at Alpha Center in Washington, DC. She has managed and conducted research on health insurance coverage and markets, the conversion of nonprofit hospitals to for-profit status, and Medicare supplemental insurance regulation, as well as provided technical assistance to state governments on related issues.

Sanford B. Herman, F.S.A., M.A.A.A., is Vice-President, Group Pricing and Standards at the Guardian Life Insurance Company and a member of the New Jersey Individual Health Coverage Program and Small Employer Health Coverage Program boards. In his position at the Guardian, Mr. Herman has oversight and responsibility for the pricing and experience analysis of all group insurance products. Prior to his current position, he directed the pricing and analysis of experience of the Guardian Portfolio Medical Group products and was responsible for all activities related to the company's managed health care product line. Mr. Herman has been involved in health insurance reform activities, assisting the Georgia Insurance Department and the Massachusetts Small Group Reform Reinsurance Pool. He is a Fellow of the Society of Actuaries (F.S.A.) and a member of the American Academy of Actuaries (M.A.A.A.). He is a Phi Beta Kappa graduate of New York University with a major in mathematics.

Steven B. Larsen, J.D., is partner in the insurance practice group at Saul Ewing LLP. Between 1997 and 2003 he was Insurance Commissioner for the state of Maryland, where he was responsible for administering state health insurance reform in the small-group and individual health insurance markets. Prior to this appointment, Commissioner Larsen had served as the chief legislative officer for the Governor of Maryland, Parris N. Glendening. He has also served as counsel and senior counsel for the USF&G Corporation, as legislative aide to a prior Maryland Governor, William Donald Schaefer, and as counsel for the Economic Matters Committee of the House of Delegates in the Maryland General Assembly. He received a Bachelor's degree in business administration from Gettysburg College, a Master's degree in politics and public policy from the Eagleton Institute of Politics, Rutgers University, and the Jurist Doctor degree from Rutgers-Camden School of Law.

M. Susan Marquis, Ph.D., is a Senior Economist at RAND, a public policy research institute. Previously, she was an economist at Research Triangle Institute, with responsibility for economic analysis of environmental policies. Dr. Marquis has an extensive record of research on consumer demand for health insurance, health plan choice, and employer-sponsored health insurance. She received her Ph.D. in economics from the University of Michigan.

Len M. Nichols, Ph.D., is Vice-President of the Center for Studying Health System Change (HSC). Previously, he served as a Principal Research Associate at the Urban Institute and has held positions as senior advisor for health policy at the Office of Management and the Budget where he oversaw cost and revenue estimates for President Clinton's Health Security Act. Dr. Nichols was a Visiting Public Health Service Fellow at the Agency for Healthcare Research and Quality, and an Associate Professor and Chair of the Department of Economics at Wellesley College. He has written and published extensively on a variety of topics, including insurance market regulation, the effect of tax policy on health insurance purchase decisions and private insurance options for Medicare. He is also a member of the Competitive Pricing Advisory Committee, a group convened by the US Department of Health and Human Services to guide attempts to begin competitive bidding for Medicare + Choice plans in select markets. Dr. Nichols earned his Ph.D. in economics from the University of Illinois, Urbana – Champaign.

Karen Pollitz, M.P.P., is a Project Director at the Georgetown University Institute for Health Care Research and Policy, where she researches health insurance reform issues as they affect consumers and patients. Ms. Pollitz's work has focused on regulation of private health coverage by federal and state government, access to affordable health insurance, managed care consumer protections, and confidentiality of medical records. As an Adjunct Professor for the Graduate Public Policy Institute at Georgetown University, she teaches graduate-level seminars on health insurance reform policy and process. Before going to Georgetown University, Ms. Pollitz served as Deputy Assistant Secretary for Health Legislation with the US Department of Health and Human Services. Karen Pollitz earned an M.P.P. from the Graduate School of Public Policy at the University of California, Berkeley, and a B.A. with Honors from Oberlin College.

Barbara Schone, Ph.D., is a senior economist in the Center for Financing, Access and Cost Trends at the Agency for Healthcare Research and Quality. Prior to this position, Dr. Schone taught in the Economics Department at Vanderbilt University. She received her Ph.D. in economics at the University of Virginia, where she was an Alfred P. Sloan Doctoral Dissertation Fellow. Dr. Schone's research focuses on the economics of health, with a interest in the link between employment and health insurance and the economics of the family, with a focus on how families make caregiving decisions for frail elderly parents. Her work has been published in the *Journal of Human Resources*, *Demography*, *Inquiry*, and *Health Affairs*. Dr. Schone is also an Adjunct Professor in the Public Policy Program at Georgetown University. In 1996 she received the New Investigator Award for Excellence in Research in Aging and Disability from the Gerontological Health Section of the American Public Health Association.

Kosali Ilayperuma Simon, Ph.D., is an Assistant Professor in the Department of Policy Analysis and Management at Cornell University. She received her B.A. in economics and German from Hamilton College and her M.A. and Ph.D. in economics from the University of Maryland at College Park. Her research and teaching interests focus on policy-oriented issues in health economics, labor economics, and public finance. Her past research has studied how state regulation of private health insurance affects the outcomes in insurance and labor markets.

Katherine Swartz, Ph.D., is a Professor in the Department of Health Policy and Management at Harvard School of Public Health, Harvard University. Her research interests focus on the population without health insurance and efforts to increase access to health care coverage, as well as health care financing and organization. Within this range of topics, she is currently examining whether regulations of insurance markets and subsidies of premiums can effectively increase access to health insurance. Professor Swartz is editor of *Inquiry*, the journal of health care provision, organization and financing. She completed her undergraduate work at MIT, and earned an M.S. and Ph.D. from the University of Wisconsin, Madison.

The editors

Alan C. Monheit, Ph.D., is Professor, School of Public Health, Department of Health Systems and Policy, School of Public Health, University of Medicine and Dentistry of New Jersey. He is also a Research Professor in the Institute for Health, Health Care Policy, and Aging Research and its Center for State Health Policy at Rutgers University. Dr. Monheit has held previous positions as Director of the Division of Social and Economic Research in the Center for Cost and Financing Studies, Agency for Healthcare Research and Quality, and as a research associate at the Boston University Health Policy Institute and the Boston University School of Medicine. His research interests include the relationship between employment and health insurance coverage, health insurance dynamics, the uninsured population, the distribution of health care expenditures and health insurance benefits, and children's access to health care. Dr. Monheit has served as a member of the President's Health Reform Task Force and in 1993 received the first Administrator's Award for Health Services Research from the Agency for Health Care Policy and Research. He is an editor and contributor to the volume *Informing American Health Care Policy: The Dynamics of Medical Expenditure and Insurance Surveys, 1997–1996*. Dr. Monheit is also a Fellow of the Employee Benefit Research Institute and an elected member of the National Academy of Social Insurance.

Joel C. Cantor, Sc.D., is Director of the Rutgers Center for State Health Policy and Professor of Public Policy at the Edward J. Bloustein School of Planning and Public Policy at Rutgers, the State University of New Jersey. Prior to joining the Rutgers faculty in February 1999, Dr Cantor served as Director of Research at the United Hospital Fund in New York City. Dr. Cantor's research has focused on issues of health care financing and delivery at the state level. His recent work includes studies of the effect of health care market competition on access to care, the organization and performance of the health care safety net for the uninsured, and the role of minority physicians in improving access to care of underserved populations. Dr. Cantor has published widely on health policy topics, and serves on the editorial board of the policy journal *Inquiry*. He received a Doctor of Science degree from Johns Hopkins University.

Preface

Although the increasing size of the uninsured population in the United States remains an ongoing public concern, there is currently little prospect of system-wide health care reform to address the failure of private health insurance markets to respond to this important policy issue. However, for nearly two decades, state governments have implemented reform of their small-group and individual health insurance markets with the intent of ensuring access to affordable and stable health care coverage. Such reform has been accompanied by keen interest from researchers and policy-makers alike as to whether this type of intervention can address the selection and pricing practices of private insurers that have been perceived as limiting the availability of coverage, especially to individuals with health problems. Policymaker interest has stimulated a variety of research on the primary impact of reform on health insurance coverage rates, for both the general population as well as those groups specifically targeted by reform, and on secondary effects of reform regarding labor market outcomes and the structure of private insurance markets. To date, however, there has been little effort to provide a critical assessment of these research findings, their applied methodologies, and the implications of such research for public policy.

The confluence of the broad interest of policymakers and researchers across the country in scrutinizing the impact of insurance regulatory reforms and the specific motivation of decision makers in New Jersey to critically revisit their own pathbreaking regulatory strategy provided the motivation for assembling the chapters in this volume. New Jersey was among the first states to implement comprehensive access and rating regulations in its individual and small-group health insurance markets. After more than a decade of experience with reform, New Jersey policymakers are revisiting that state's regulatory regime. New Jersey's regulators and insurance carriers have been particularly receptive to scrutiny of that state's efforts to encourage affordable access to individual health insurance. Shortly after implementing its major reforms in 1993, and again in 2002, state officials and participating insurance carriers made themselves and their data available to academic researchers. As well, stimulated by their interest in improving the effectiveness of regulation in the individual and small-group markets, New Jersey regulators eagerly collaborated with researchers at the Rutgers University Center for State Health Policy in 2003 to convene the experts represented in this volume to help them understand the impact of insurance market reform across the states. This close collaboration between policy researchers and regulators and insurers provides an essential platform for assuring the relevance of researchers' efforts and the effective translation of their findings into policy and practices.

The goal of this collection of essays on state insurance market reform is to fill an important gap in our knowledge. Through the efforts of a group of nationally recognized health economists and individuals with unique expertise in the provision, regulation, and impact of private health insurance, we have assembled a broad and diverse set of essays that will help to put the research findings in perspective and that will enlighten readers as to the critical methodological requirements necessary to identify a causal relationship between reform and outcomes of interest. It is our hope that these contributions will also serve to illuminate the sometimes contentious debate over the impact of reform, provide insights which will be of value to both researchers and policymakers alike, stimulate consideration of ways to improve reform's performance, and raise possible policy responses to the shortcomings of reform. Above all, we hope that this volume will contribute to a dialogue between researchers and policymakers as to ways to address the equity and efficiency implications of disparities health insurance coverage among the US population and the appropriate balance between regulatory efforts and private market activity in helping to address this important welfare issue.

Alan C. Monheit
Joel C. Cantor

Acknowledgments

Assembling a volume on a subject as compelling and contentious as state health insurance market reform is an ambitious and often sobering task. Our efforts in doing so reflect the contributions of numerous individuals whose hard work, financial and collegial support, and good humor kept our project on track and our efforts in perspective. We wish to acknowledge their input to this challenging process.

We are grateful to the contributors to this volume for their willingness to tackle the various assigned topics, their receptiveness to our editorial suggestions, and above all the thoughtfulness and quality of their efforts. This volume reflects the fruits of their intellectual efforts and their many original insights and experiences as students of state health insurance market reform. We have learned much from their efforts.

The papers in this volume were based on presentations in April 2003 at an Expert Panel convened by the Center for State Health Policy and New Jersey Department of Banking and Insurance. Financial support for the Expert Panel was provided under a State Planning Grant to the State of New Jersey from the US Health Resources and Services Administration. Additional financial support for this volume was provided under a grant to the Center for State Health Policy by the Robert Wood Johnson Foundation. Wardell Sanders and Vicki Mangiaracina of the New Jersey Department Banking and Insurance were partners with us in shaping the agenda for the Expert Panel and, ultimately, the selection of topics and authors for this volume.

Finally, we are indebted to Lori Glickman for her diligence, hard work, skill, and high standards in assembling and formatting the manuscript, figures, and tables. Margaret Koller provided assistance at every point of the editorial process and served as a contact with each of our contributors, managing to keep the project on schedule. We are grateful to both for the seriousness with which they approached their responsibilities.

A.C.M.
J.C.C.

Abbreviations

BCBS Plans	Blue Cross and Blue Shield Plans
COBRA	Consolidated Omnibus Budget Reconciliation Act 1985
CPS	Current Population Survey
DD estimator	Difference-in-differences estimator
DDD estimator	Difference-in-differences-in-differences estimator
HCFA	Health Care Financing Administration (renamed the Center for Medicare and Medicaid Services)
HIPAA	Health Insurance Portability and Accountability Act of 1996
IHCP	New Jersey's Individual Health Coverage Program
MEPS	Medical Expenditure Panel Survey
NEHIS	National Employer Health Insurance Survey
NMES	National Medical Expenditure Survey
NSAF	National Survey of America's Families
SIPP	Survey of Income and Program Participation

1 Introduction

Alan C. Monheit and Joel C. Cantor

Setting the stage

In his seminal work on the distinguishing characteristics of medical care markets written in 1963, Kenneth Arrow asserted that "the welfare case for insurance policies of all sorts is overwhelming. It follows that the government should undertake insurance in those cases where this market, for whatever reason, fails to emerge."[1] As if prompted by Arrow's observation, the federal government shortly thereafter established the Medicare and Medicaid programs to address the failure of health insurance markets to emerge for the elderly and the poor and disabled. However, over the ensuing four decades, and despite a series of legislative proposals from Republicans and Democrats alike, the United States has made scant progress toward the goal of universal health care coverage. The most recent comprehensive federal proposal, President Clinton's Health Security Act of 1993, failed to achieve a political consensus, igniting a contentious public debate over the appropriate way to expand coverage, organize health insurance markets, and design a comprehensive yet affordable benefit package.

While the Clinton administration successfully sponsored the 1997 State Children's Health Insurance Program (S-CHIP), the largest expansion of coverage for low-income children since the enactment of Medicaid, important gaps in coverage remain for significant numbers of American families, especially in the current environment of high and accelerating health insurance premiums. Indeed, in 2002, the number and percent of non-elderly uninsured Americans stood at 43.6 million and 15.2 percent respectively, an increase of nearly 3.4 million persons over the prior year (Mills and Bhandari 2003). With large federal budget deficits forecast for at least the next decade, it remains questionable at best whether the federal government can be an effective catalyst for enhanced access to private or public coverage, let alone comprehensive health care reform.

Apart from efforts towards system-wide reform, the federal government has most recently intervened in private health insurance markets to assure the continuity of coverage for persons with employment-based health insurance through the 1996 Health Insurance Portability and

Accountability Act (HIPAA) and a decade earlier through the 1985 Consolidated Omnibus Budget Reconciliation Act (COBRA). However, these laws have had little direct effect on the uninsured since they target individuals who already hold insurance as well as those whose coverage status has changed because of a specifically defined event. In addition, COBRA is only applicable for workers in firms of twenty or more employees. Thus, it fails to address changes in health insurance status among particularly vulnerable employees: those who obtain coverage from very small firms. Moreover, these interventions do little with regard to disparities in the price of coverage for individuals with otherwise similar health-related characteristics but whose employment circumstances have been arguably classified as high risk. Finally, both HIPAA and COBRA were not intended to address the questionable pricing practices used by insurers regarding the access to and subsequent renewal of coverage to persons who have experienced a costly medical event.[2]

With little prospect of a federally sponsored system-wide reform on the horizon, policymakers and researchers have developed a keen interest in incremental efforts by states to reform their health insurance markets. Since the late 1980s, over forty states have adopted some form of small-group market reform, while twenty-five states have implemented reform of their individual health insurance markets.[3] The impetus to such reform reflects a number of factors. Most prominent has been the perception of insurance market failure in the small-group and individual markets that has been fueled by a number of questionable and exclusionary insurer practices regarding the issuance, renewal, and pricing of policies. Among the practices typically cited are the aggressive use of medical underwriting and pre-existing condition exclusions; durational rating practices (in which low premiums are initially offered then increased dramatically at the first sign of unfavorable claims experience); tier rating (whereby insurers reclassify groups with unexpected medical costs to a higher rating group); the redlining of particular industries and occupations; and more subtle efforts to "cherry pick" or "cream skim" the best health risks (Hall 1992, 1994).

Next, as Mark Hall (1992) has observed, interest in reform has also been stimulated by the health insurance industry itself . As early as 1988, the Health Insurance Association of America (HIAA) recognized the need for fundamental reform in the small-group market to address the aggressive selection practices of commercial insurers and produced model legislation in February 1991. The National Association of Insurance Commissioners (NAIC), representing state insurance regulators, had also produced a model reform proposal in December 1990 for rating and renewability provisions (endorsed by the Blue Cross Association) and a year later created model legislation for guaranteed issue and reinsurance (Hall 1992). Such models have served as a valuable template for states designing their own reform provisions. Hall (1992) also notes that small-group reform focused on a significant political constituency, one that comprised at least a quarter of all uninsured persons and that was experiencing an erosion in their rate of coverage as well as in its value. Further, to the extent that reform incorporated reinsurance provisions, no major stakeholders in the small-group or individual insurance markets were likely to be seriously harmed by reform.

Market reform legislation was also attractive from at least two other perspectives. Since reform sought to constrain insurer practices by establishing rules of acceptable carrier behavior, its implicit emphasis on voluntarism on the demand side stood in stark contrast to more controversial proposals to mandate employer and individual coverage. Moreover, from a public financing perspective, market reform legislation was largely off-budget and thus required little in the way of direct government outlays. Among states that found reform to be sufficiently attractive to implement were those in adequate fiscal health, states with the capacity to administer reform, those having higher proportions of their populations uninsured, and those whose neighboring states adopted small market reform (Stream 1999).

The intent and challenge of state insurance market reform

The intent of state health insurance market reform has been relatively straightforward: to assure access to affordable health insurance by mitigating questionable selection and pricing practices by insurers. Reform has sought to achieve this goal through the guaranteed issuance and renewal of coverage to small firms and persons seeking individual coverage; by relaxing constraints on access to coverage imposed by pre-existing health conditions (typically limiting the length of waiting and look-back periods) and through provisions to enhance the portability of coverage; and by addressing disparities in the cost of coverage between high- and low-risk groups through the use of rating reforms encompassing pure and modified community rating, limits on the permissible range of premiums, and by constraints on the rate of premium growth. By reducing the disparity in premiums by enrollee health risk, reform has also played a redistributive role, effectuating the transfer of implicit subsidies from low- to high-risk enrollees.[4]

In essence, state reform has taken on the rather daunting challenge of trying to assure both *efficiency and equity* in the provision of private health insurance. From an efficiency perspective, reform has sought to create a market environment in which insurers would compete on the basis of health plan cost and quality through improved risk management rather than through favorable risk selection (Hall 1992). From an equity perspective, reform has sought to encourage a retreat from the commodification of health care and health insurance and to promote an alternative vision in which the distribution of coverage is consistent with principles of social solidarity and mutual aid rather than actuarial fairness (Stone 1993; Oliver and Fiedler 1997). Given these conflicting objectives, the challenge confronting state insurance reform has been to achieve an acceptable tradeoff between efficiency and equity, one that minimizes any unintended consequences for enrollee and insurer welfare and preserves insurance market stability. An example will bring this challenge into sharp relief: as rate-setting provisions constrain the use of risk-adjusted premiums, low-risk individuals are likely to suffer welfare losses, high-risk individuals are likely to gain, the risk composition of the insurance pool is likely to change, and consequently, insurers may find themselves compelled to take on substandard health risks who yield insufficient premium income. Thus the changes brought about by reform are unlikely to be Pareto optimal unless accompanied by premium subsidies and other financing mechanisms that allow healthy enrollees, insurers, and perhaps the more general population to share in the monetary consequences of the new risks confronting insurers. In light of such conflicting objectives, a compelling issue for public policy is whether states have been successful in achieving reform goals or whether reform has yielded unintended consequences severe enough to threaten market stability and create welfare losses for current enrollees and insurers.

With increasing attention directed to market-based solutions to address the lack of health insurance, understanding the effects of state insurance reform has taken on new saliency. In particular, the success of proposals to expand coverage to the uninsured through tax credits or other subsidies (e.g., employment-based premium support programs) requires targeted populations to have access to affordable coverage, either in the individual or small-group markets. Moreover, interest in the effectiveness of state health policies such as insurance market reform is also relevant in the context of the federal devolution of health policy responsibility to state governments (Stream 1999). Finally, those advocating the dismantling of the current system of employment-based coverage and replacing it with a competitive system of individually purchased coverage require that carriers adhere to a set of rules that promote fair price and quality competition. Whether reform efforts have created a market environment that can support such policy approaches remains a critical question in assessing the likely success of market-based efforts to expand health insurance coverage.

As the above suggests, there is much at stake in empirical evaluations of the impact of reform. At issue is whether government intervention in private insurance markets can achieve significant gains in insurance coverage without threatening market stability and whether reform can create a market environment conducive to voluntary efforts to expand coverage. Moreover, given the variation across states in the presence of reform and in its differing components, it remains to be seen as to whether empirical tests can assess the comparative effectiveness of specific reform provisions and the various reform packages. As the evidence collected in this volume illustrates, such evaluations confront a number of important conceptual, design and data challenges that must be addressed in order to answer these compelling questions.

Purpose of the volume

Since the late 1990s, a number of papers evaluating the effectiveness of state health insurance reform have appeared in technical health services research and policy journals, economics journals, book chapters, or as unpublished reports. To date, however, there has not been a unified effort to critically evaluate the extant research on reform, to examine the methodological limitations and challenges to empirical research, or to draw implications regarding the effectiveness of specific reform provisions. Perhaps most important, there has not been a serious effort to assess more globally whether reform is a viable and effective policy instrument or whether modifications to reform or alternative policy options will improve reform outcomes. Such an effort requires not only an assessment of the quantitative empirical findings but also the perspective of individuals who have had first-hand experience implementing reform, providing information to potential market entrants, or directly monitoring the effects of reform.

The intent of this book is to provide a critical assessment of the current state of knowledge on insurance market reform that will be accessible to both researchers and policymakers. Its emphasis focuses primarily on economic analyses and econometric studies that have examined reform through empirical analyses using national or state-specific data. In this regard, the evidence and assessments compiled in this volume depart sharply from the very important qualitative and case-specific studies that have come before. We would be remiss by not acknowledging the importance of this work in describing the institutional features and foundations of reform and more generally educating researchers as to the role played by key participants in reform activity (e.g., agents and brokers, regulators, insurers, etc.) and the subtle behavioral responses that could compromise the intent and effectiveness of reform.[5]

The chapters of this volume were commissioned as papers for a conference on state insurance market reform held in April 2003, jointly sponsored by the Center for State Health Policy (CSHP) at Rutgers, the State University of New Jersey and the New Jersey Department and Banking and Insurance. The conference assembled a group of nationally recognized scholars, policy analysts, insurers, and state officials to evaluate the impact and current status of insurance market reform. CSHP commissioned papers by these conference participants to assess research findings on state health insurance market reform, to consider the evidence in terms of its face validity, expectations regarding reform, intended and unintended effects, methodological challenges, and relevance and implications for policy. These papers represent the results of this effort and provide a scholarly assessment that will be accessible to policy analysts and researchers alike.

The chapters

Part I Critical evaluation of research findings

Small-group reform

Most empirical research evaluating the impact of insurance market reform has focused on reform in the small employer group market. Chapter 2 by Kosali Simon provides a comprehensive review of this literature. Simon begins by discussing the underlying rationale for small-group reform and describes the set of policy instruments used in its implementation. These typically include provisions to ensure access to coverage and restrict variation in premiums. Simon describes the variation in reform legislation across states and notes that a particular challenge to comparing and assessing results is the fact that empirical work contains a variety of definitions of reform prevalence and stringency. She also draws a sharp distinction between the realistic and unrealistic expectations for reform. Simon asserts that reform could not realistically expect to narrow rates of coverage or premium levels between small and large firms or even control changes in the level of premiums over time. She points to the possibility that reform access provisions could very well alter the risk composition of the small-group market toward poor health risks, yielding implications for the level of premiums faced by small employers and their employees. For example, if reform successfully enhances access to coverage by poorer health risks relative to standard risks, and if variation in premiums are minimized through provisions such as pure community rating, average premium *levels* will increase and may yield the unintended effect of reducing market participation by better health risks (who withdraw from the market in response to the higher premiums). Thus, Simon argues, reasonable expectations for reform include a reduction in the variation and volatility of premiums across small firms and overtime within a particular firm, and to mitigate a number of questionable underwriting practices by insurers which have led to outright denials of coverage and excessive year-to-year increases in premiums for some small firms.

Simon observes that research has primarily focused on assessing reform's impact on outcomes related to health insurance status (e.g., policyholder status, coverage status, uninsured rates, and offers of coverage) and to a much more limited extent on premiums for small employer coverage and on market structure. However, since the provision of a non-pecuniary employment benefit such as health insurance can also affect employee wage levels, hours of work, and employment opportunities at small firms, Simon also notes that a small set of research efforts have focused on these secondary labor market effects of reform. On balance, her assessment suggests that despite analysts' use of different data sets, units of observation, classification of reform provisions, and methodological approaches, research on small-group reform has generally reached as consistent and robust set of findings. She concludes that while reform has not caused chaos in the small-group market, such research has found little impact of reform on these outcome measures. However, some findings suggest that reform may have led to unintended and differential effects according to employee health risk, improving coverage rates for high-risk employees relative to low-risk workers.

Individual market reform

Currently, only a small fraction of the non-elderly US population participates in the individual health insurance market. However, this market has figured prominently in policy discussions as an alternative to the employment-based insurance system, as a vehicle for expanding health insurance coverage through tax credits, and as a means of inducing greater competition in the provision of private insurance and expanding coverage options for consumers. While a number of states have implemented reform in this market to address issues of questionable insurer selection and pricing practices, assessing the impact of such reform efforts is challenging, for it must account for the fragile nature of this market and its sensitivity to trends in national and regional economic conditions. Whether state reform can help to stabilize this market by providing more individuals with access to affordable coverage is thus a critical policy concern.

Deborah Chollet acknowledges these considerations in Chapter 3. As described by Chollet, the individual insurance market is a small, highly concentrated, and potentially volatile residual market characterized by high premiums. Enrollees in the individual market are a more diverse group than those with employment-based coverage and tend to hold coverage for short periods of time. She notes (while raising methodological concerns) that limited research indicates that demand for individual coverage is also price-inelastic so that reform would have to yield large premium reductions to elicit a sizable enrollment response. Finally, Chollet also asserts that, in theory, the individual insurance market is far more susceptible to adverse selection than the employment-based market leading insurers to engage in favorable risk selection. However, she observes that there is little empirical evidence of adverse selection in this market, a finding that may reflect measurement and other methodological limitations.

Chollet's review of the few quantitative studies that assess the impact of individual market reforms reveals findings that are generally mixed and inconsistent. Some work on the impact of access reforms (e.g., guaranteed issue and renewal; constraints on the use of pre-existing condition) indicate that such interventions increased uninsured rates and reduced the likelihood of individual coverage, while other studies suggest little impact of reform on coverage rates or face difficulty attributing causality from reform to changes in coverage. Work assessing the relationship between access reforms and changes in market structure and insurer concentration also yield mixed results. While there are few studies that empirically assess the impact of premium regulation in the individual market on coverage rates, the author's own work suggests that more restrictive and comprehensive rate bands may have the unintended effect of reducing coverage among healthy adults (a finding comparable to research on the impact of small-group reform). Chollet also observes that the few qualitative studies of state experiences with reform also yield uncertainty regarding reform impacts on coverage, market structure, and the supply of health insurance products. She concludes by noting that it may be unrealistic to expect individual market reform to yield lower premiums or increased coverage, given the tendency for insurers to offer coverage at relatively high premiums in order to slow enrollment in an uncertain regulatory environment.

Part II Responses to findings on insurance market reform

Establishing a causal relationship between the presence of reform and specific outcomes of interest presents an important challenge to researchers, one that is compounded by data imperfections and limitations, alternative ways to characterize insurance market reform, and varying model specifications. Moreover, the quasi-experimental approaches used by a number of studies are based on a strong set of assumptions and selection of study periods that are frequently constrained by available data. While researchers strive to identify causality and obtain a set of plausible and unbiased estimates, policymakers and nonspecialists are generally unfamiliar with estimation methodologies and primarily concerned with whether the research yields a reliable set of empirical estimates that can inform public policy. Although their perspectives may differ, researchers and policymakers alike need a guide to more effectively assess the credibility of the research, to help put the research findings in perspective, and to provide a more general *caveat emptor* to consumers of the research. Chapters 4 by Thomas Buchmueller and 5 by Barbara Schone seek to fill this important role.

What can we learn from the research?

Thomas Buchmueller's chapter provides a general assessment of the quality of research findings on reform and the care that is necessary to assign a causal relationship between reform and outcomes of interest. He begins by reviewing two widely circulated evaluations of insurance market reform in New York in which each study concluded that reform was responsible for reduced rates of insurance coverage, a finding with very serious policy implications. He then reveals the critical flaws and omissions in each study's design that contributed to this inappropriate conclusion. Through this example, Buchmueller illustrates the challenges to identifying a true causal relationship as well as a caution to policymakers who wish to draw upon such research.

Buchmueller then proceeds to identify a number of critical design challenges that researchers confront in empirical assessments of reform's impact. These include the difficulty of establishing the counterfactual to reform – that is, what would have happened had reform not been implemented – through the use of comparable set of non-reform states as a control group; the sensitivity of estimates of reform's impact to the choice of pre- and post-reform time periods; and the use of an appropriately designated treatment group that has been targeted by reform. He notes that researchers generally fail to justify these choices or investigate the sensitivity of results to alternative target and control groups or time periods. Other key considerations cited by Buchmueller are whether empirical results, particularly in the quasi-natural experiments used to identify reform effects, are driven by changes in the treatment group (rather than the control group) and whether reform has a theoretically plausible effect on target groups according to health risk.

Buchmueller concludes that small-group reform on average had generally no impact on employee insurance status and considers three possible explanations for this lack of impact. First, he observes that insurer underwriting practices had very little, if any, impact on the ability of small firms to obtain coverage for their employees, so that the potential impact of reform on such practices may have been quite limited. Next, he suggests that in many states, reform may have had only a marginal effect on insurer behavior. He notes that states with rating rules based on particular demographic characteristics still offer insurers considerable flexibility to vary rates within specific demographic cells; that regulations limiting guaranteed issue to one or two plans may allow such plans to be separately rated to reflect the higher cost of their enrollees; and that insurers may not market such plans aggressively. Finally, Buchmueller notes that while coverage rates may not have changed in response to reform, enrollees may have sorted into alternative and less costly health care coverage rather than choosing to abandon coverage.

Buchmueller completes his chapter by asking whether the high expectations for reform held by its proponents were reasonable. Here he notes that demand-side factors may be more responsible for the high and rising uninsured rates than are the supply-side constraints addressed by reform. Nevertheless, since reform effects are at least theoretically possible, he asserts that there is a rationale for the empirical work undertaken and for recognizing the challenges in conducting careful and objective research.

A critical assessment of methodologies

As Barbara Schone observes, confidence in empirical estimates of the impact of reform on health insurance status is especially compelling since economic theory can only provide ambiguous predictions. With much empirical work indicating that reform, at best, has had only a modest effect on coverage, it becomes essential to consider whether the methodologies employed are capable of identifying causality and producing unbiased estimates of reform's impact. Shone's objective is to explore the potential for such bias in the alternative estimation strategies that have been used to identify the impact of small-group reform.

In assessing the various empirical approaches, Schone draws the distinction between "first-generation" and "second-generation" studies of reform. She notes that first-generation studies were subject to potential bias from unobserved or omitted factors (e.g., economic factors) potentially associated with both the presence of reform and health insurance outcomes. As a result, a finding of a correlation between the presence of reform and the outcome of interest might not necessarily reflect a causal relationship but instead, the impact of omitted or unobserved factors. As Schone observes, second-generation studies have applied more sophisticated, quasi-experimental methods to control for such influences (through difference-in-differences methods and difference-in-differences-in-differences study designs). Such approaches treat reform states as an "experimental" group and non-reform states as a "control" group and examine change in specific outcomes pre- and post-reform. Despite such innovations, Schone asserts that even these techniques could be subject to biases and proceeds to discuss a range of relevant methodological issues.

Factors cited by Schone as having the potential to contaminate estimates of reform impact in both first- and second-generation studies are policy endogeneity (e.g., observed or unobserved factors associated with the adoption of reform that are also correlated with the outcome studied); policy timing and type of data used (which are typically limit assessments to short-run effects of reform and preclude a distinction between transitory and permanent effects) ; the choice of pre- and post-reform periods (which fail to capture behavior in anticipation of reform); potential multicollinearity (due to the bundling of specific reform provisions which precludes identifying the precise causal mechanism of reform); data limitations that preclude appropriate measurement of the risk profile of a firm's workforce; and adequate sample size (the number of small-firm employees in reform states) to ensure statistical precision. Schone also identifies methodological issues unique to second-generation studies. These include assumptions regarding the constancy of the composition of treatment and control groups over time; whether groups designated as controls (i.e., larger firms) do indeed make good controls (since they may be insulated from the economic fluctuations that affect small firms); and whether it is safe to assume the controls are unaffected by reform.

Schone's discussion also identifies several promising econometric approaches with the potential to improve the robustness of reform estimates and that provide information on the distributional consequences of reform. She concludes her chapter with suggestions for approaches to research that might constitute a third generation of reform studies.

Part III Perspective from the field

Does the empirical evidence regarding reform's impact resonate with individuals who have had practical experience with reform? In this part, three contributions provide unique perspectives on this issue: those of an insurance executive, a regulator, and a consumer advocate. Their chapters provide a window to the reality of reform implementation and offer insights as to what might best be expected from reform and to the interpretation of empirical findings on the effectiveness of reform.

An insurer's perspective

Offering the perspective of an insurance executive, Sanford Herman discusses in Chapter 6 the evolution of reform in the context of changing insurer behavior in the employment-based and individual health insurance markets and the problems posed by rising health insurance premiums. Herman's essay echos an insight provided by Thomas Buchmueller: that market reforms are largely supply-side measures that rely on voluntary responses by employers and individuals to the enhanced availability of coverage. As Herman observes, such voluntarism may work well in a period of stable or slowly rising health insurance costs. However, when insurance markets face high and rapidly growing premiums and reform measures constrain the ability of insurers to differentiate premiums according to individual health risk, it should not be surprising that reform appears to be an ineffective policy tool to reduce the size of the uninsured population as much of the empirical work suggests. More specifically, Herman asserts that a primary reason for the lack of success with reform has been its failure to address the reality that targeted groups are either unable or unwilling to pay for coverage. Given the limits of voluntarism in both the small-group and individual insurance markets, Herman proceeds to outline a proposal for an alternative to reform based on a system of mandated health insurance benefits funded by required employer and employee contributions (assisted by general revenues) in the small-group market and income-related subsidies in the individual market.

An insurance commissioner's perspective

As insurance commissioner for the State of Maryland, Steven Larsen was responsible for overseeing Maryland's small-group and individual market reforms. In Chapter 7, Larsen addresses the political realities of administering reform in each market. He notes that a particular challenge to managing reform in the small-group market is the continuing pressure to expand the breadth of benefits while maintaining affordable coverage. Larsen cites the intense pressure to incorporate mandated benefits in the Maryland's benefit package and the tradeoff in terms of changes in cost-sharing provisions that are necessary to meet limits on annual premium increases. Despite such pressure, Larsen asserts that Maryland's small-group market reform has generally been viewed as successful, in terms of increasing access to coverage for employees of small firms, the number of covered lives, and keeping premium levels below those of comparable reform states. However, the small-group market faces continuing challenges from the general acceleration in health care costs.

Larsen is less sanguine regarding reform in the individual market. He characterizes the market as highly concentrated and noncompetitive, one that has been subject to a combination of large premium increases, stricter underwriting rules (compared to the small-group market), and exclusionary riders. However, he also observes that Maryland has implemented a new high-risk pool as a means of reducing the cost pressures experienced by the individual market. While Larsen notes that it is difficult to discern a relationship between reform and a reduction in Maryland's uninsured population, he believes that small-group reform has been effective in increasing the number of small businesses offering coverage in the state.

Protecting consumers

In Chapter 8 Karen Pollitz draws lessons from her experience researching the impact of reform on consumers and patients. Specifically, she addresses the question of whether access to affordable insurance is feasible and sustainable under insurance market reform. Focusing on the individual health insurance market, Pollitz asserts that its weaknesses – small size, unsubsidized premiums, voluntary participation, high turnover, and potential for adverse selection – cast doubt as to whether this market can meet reform's goals of accessible, affordable, and adequate coverage for all potential entrants. Instead, she notes that such incremental reform is likely to yield winners and losers, resulting in a political determination of the acceptable tradeoffs and mix of winners and losers.

Pollitz describes five different approaches to state reform in the individual insurance market including states with comprehensive reform (e.g., guaranteed issue, standardized insurance products, limits on pre-existing conditions, pure community rating), those with portability protections, those that have designated a carrier of last resort, those with only high-risk pools, and states with minimalist reform (protections granted under 1996 HIPAA legislation). She notes that in states without comprehensive reform, underwriting practices significantly limit access to standard coverage at advertised rates for persons in less than perfect health as well as for those with minor health conditions. She also characterizes the shortcomings of reform in states without comprehensive provisions and describes a number of other state strategies that have been applied to the individual market.

Pollitz concludes by calling for a comprehensive analyses of different state reform efforts in the individual market. Absent such an evaluation, she observes that the current debate over reform will continue to be quite political, contentious, and based upon inaccurate and exaggerated claims. The politicalization of individual reform, she asserts, does not serve the public well, since it fails to address the tradeoffs and real costs involved in relaxing or in even repealing reform.

Part IV Reforming insurance market reform: What are the possibilities? What are the alternatives?

The evidence assembled by Kosali Simon and Deborah Chollet strongly indicates that reform has had little impact on expanding health insurance coverage in the small-group and individual market. This raises the compelling issue of whether there are ways to make reform more effective or whether alternatives to reform might prove more successful in achieving desired outcomes. Three chapters in this part directly address these issues. In Chapter 9 Susan Marquis considers whether there are ways to improve the effectiveness of reform and outlines a number of potential reform options, especially as regards payments to health plans. In contrast, Len Nichols and Kathy Swartz each focus on a specific alternative to reform. In Chapter 10 Nichols develops the theory and supporting empirical evidence for a system of risk-based premium subsidies for high risks that allow standard risks to pay no more than their actuarially fair rate. Swartz, in Chapter 11, proposes the use of reinsurance pools to compensate those insurers who draw high-cost health risks. Both Marquis and Swartz share the view that, by constraining the supply price available to insurers, reform has neglected insurer concerns regarding adverse selection. Alternatively, Nichols notes that by raising the costs of coverage to good risks, premium regulation has result in an implicit tax on such enrollees and a transfer to poor risks and has contributed to insurance market instability. None of the authors believes that reform, as currently implemented, can be an effective tool to significantly expand coverage for the uninsured.

Improving market reform through alternative policy tools

Susan Marquis's Chapter 9 begins by raising the issue of whether insurer concerns regarding adverse selection are real or simply misplaced. While the evidence on adverse selection is arguably mixed, Marquis notes that regulations which limit insurer underwriting and pricing practices lead carriers to seek other methods to favorably select enrollees. Marquis proceeds to thoroughly evaluate several mechanisms – premium risk adjustment, high-risk pools, and purchasing cooperatives – that might be used in conjunction with market reform to overcome insurer responses.

Marquis's discussion of risk adjustment identifies a number of strategies for consideration. She reviews the well known difficulties in implementing prospective risk adjustment (paucity of detailed data, ability of risk adjustment models to adequately explain variation in costs) and explores several variations in risk adjustment methodologies, including retrospective risk sharing, threshold reinsurance, proportional risk sharing, risk sharing restricted to high-risk cases, and condition-specific risk sharing. While each of these approaches confronts technical, and in some cases political, obstacles to implementation, she notes that simulation analyses suggest that such strategies have the potential to greatly reduce adverse selection.

While risk-adjusted premiums may yield a more equitable distribution of payments across health plans and thus address inefficient favorable selection by insurers, Marquis echoes the concerns expressed earlier by Thomas Buchmueller and Sanford Herman that reform has neglected the demand price of insurance. She observes that the supply price paid to an insurer for a particular enrollee need not be the same as the demand price faced by a consumer. Consequently, the effect of risk adjustment on coverage rates will depend on efforts to make the demand price attractive to potential enrollees, such as through the use of subsidies and external financing of a portion of the risk-adjusted payments. Finally, Marquis considers the role for high-risk pools and purchasing cooperatives in insurance market reform. While she views limited potential for the former, she sees a more viable role for risk pools, since they reduce insurer incentives to select favorable risks and can shift the burden of paying for risks away from low-risk enrollees and the specific market. However, given the experience of risk pools to date, she recognizes that substantial subsidies will be required to make them a viable policy instrument. Marquis concludes by noting that a variety of strategies may be required to expand coverage among the uninsured.

A system of risk-based premium subsidies

As Len Nichols observes in Chapter 10, reform has sought to achieve the three specific goals of more stable and less variable premiums, more stable and sustainable insurance markets, and affordable coverage, especially for persons in poor health. However, Nichols asserts, in efforts to meet these goals, reformers confront an inherent tension: stable and affordable premiums and markets are sought by imposing an implicit premium tax on good risks and making implicit transfers that reduce the premiums paid by poor risks. Although these taxes and transfers are achieved through restrictions that constrain premiums from their unregulated *laissez-faire* levels, Nichols notes that other features of reform, such as limits on pre-existing condition exclusions and the guaranteed issue and renewability of policies, have a similar effect. As a result, reform creates incentives for good risks to disenroll from the small-group and individual markets, thus threatening premium levels and market stability.

Given this generic problem, Nichols proposes a system of risk-based subsidies that he believes will prove to be more equitable and efficient in achieving increased coverage than current reform provisions. Under his proposal, standard health risks pay premiums that are no more than their actuarially fair costs while individuals in poor health or those with low incomes pay no more than the community rate. The latter groups, however, are subsidized for the difference between the community rate and their expected medical care costs through general tax revenues. In essence, the system of subsidies is external to the insurance market and does not distort the premiums to be paid by standard health risks.

Nichols provides a theoretical description of the welfare implications of such a system and presents an empirical simulation of its implications for costs and coverage. The results suggest that compared to either a *laissez-faire* or a community-rated system of premiums, a system of risk-based subsidies has the potential to cover nearly all the uninsured. In contrast, an unregulated *laissez-faire* insurance market achieves the highest level of net economic welfare (since no subsidies are required) but the cost of this greater efficiency is the improved equity and market stability that are achieved under a risk-based subsidy system. Nichols concludes by noting that risk-based premiums are a viable alternative to traditional reform provisions should society find the equity implications of an unregulated system unacceptable and have the political will to finance the required subsidies.

Reinsurance as a policy response

Katherine Swartz begins Chapter 11 by noting that a primary reason for insurance market reform has been to address the market failure brought about by problems of asymmetric information regarding health risk. Since potential enrollees have more information than insurers regarding their health risks, Swartz asserts that insurers will compete on the basis of favorable risk selection rather than through price or product quality, and that such behavior will result in a socially inefficient use of resources. Although reform efforts have sought to enhance high-risk individuals' access to coverage by eroding carriers' underwriting and selection practices, Swartz asserts that such efforts have done little to allay carrier fears of adverse selection and thus have perpetuated favorable risk selection through more subtle methods.

To address these concerns, Swartz proposes that state or federal governments implement a retrospective reinsurance system which would compensate carriers in the non-group market for most of the costs of enrolling very high-cost individuals. Under this scheme, the share of high-cost expenditures borne by the government could vary over different expenditure thresholds, thus reducing the risks to specific carriers. Such reinsurance could lead to lower carrier-specific premiums since it would shift the burden of the costs of extremely high-risk persons from healthier enrollees in particular health plans to the general tax-paying population. Lower premiums, in turn, would contribute to insurance market stability by encouraging the enrollment and retention of low-risk individuals. Swartz also believes that the retrospective nature of reisurance will lead to other advantages including an accurate assessment of carrier burden due to high-cost enrollees and more attention to the management of persons with high-cost illnesses.

Swartz draws two key lessons from past reform efforts. First, she notes that carriers' ability to effectively engage in favorable risk selection will depend on the extent of reform regulation but that more extensive reform will impose costs on low-risk enrollees through reduced plan choice and increased premiums. Thus reform involves a tradeoff between the interests of high and low-risk individuals. Next, she asserts that public policy may be more successful in achieving premium stability and carrier participation when private as well as public policymakers help to design the regulations. She notes that private policymakers have a stake in the outcome, may be better able to anticipate carrier responses to particular regulations, and thus can help to design regulations to achieve a desired response. Swartz concludes by emphasizing the importance of addressing carrier fears of adverse risk selection in order to achieve the goals of enhanced coverage and efficient and stable market behavior and by urging serious consideration of government reinsurance mechanisms to achieve this goal.

Conclusions

The chapters of this volume provide a very broad and diverse set of perspectives on research findings, methodological challenges, and policy implications that we believe are critical to understanding and interpreting research findings on the impact of state insurance market reform. We hope that this collection will help to clarify the debate over the impact of reform and provide readers with new insights regarding research findings and methods, policy implications, and alternative approaches to achieving reform's goal of expanded health insurance coverage. Perhaps most important, we hope that this work will resonate with researchers and policymakers alike: that it will encourage the former group to pursue new and creative evaluations of the impact of insurance market reform along the many dimensions described by our authors, and that it will challenge policymakers and analysts to continue to seek initiatives that address issues of equity and efficiency in the provision of affordable and sustainable health insurance coverage.

Notes

1 Arrow (1963). Of course, in response to Arrow's assertion, Mark Pauly (1968) has argued that in some instances health insurance may also lead to a loss in efficiency through a moral hazard welfare loss.
2 HIPAA does guarantee the issue and renewal of coverage to small firms. However, HIPAA and COBRA do not address the affordability of coverage. For example, COBRA enrollees may be required to pay as much as 102 percent of their former group's premium, which may be well in excess of their out-of-pocket premium costs when employed.
3 See, for example, Chapter 2 by Kosali Simon, Chapter 4 by Thomas C. Buchmueller, Chapter 8 by Karen Pollitz, and Chapter 5 by Barbara Schone.
4 In this regard, reform departs from Arrow's (1963: 963–964) admonition that to achieve its full social benefit insurance requires a "maximum possible discrimination of risks" whereby individuals with a greater incidence of illness pay higher premiums. That is, reform seeks to achieve its access goals directly through the price system rather than through actuarially fair premiums and accompanying health or income-related premium subsidies.
5 Here we refer to work by Mark Hall, Karen Pollitz, and Katherine Swartz and Deborah Garnick.

References

Arrow, Kenneth, J. (1963) "Uncertainty and the Welfare Economics of Medical Care." *American Economic Review*, 54 (December): 971–973.

Hall, M.A. (1992) "The Political Economics of Health Insurance Market Reforms." *Health Affairs*, 11 (summer): 108–124.

Hall, M.A. (1994) *Reforming Private Health Insurance*. Washington, DC: American Enterprise Institute.

Mills, R.J. and Bhandari, S. (2003) "Health Insurance Coverage in the United States: 2002." Washington, DC: US Bureau of the Census.

Oliver, T.R. and Fiedler, R.M. (1997) "State Government and Health Insurance Market Reform" in Howard M. Leichter (ed.) *Health Policy Reform in America: Innovations from the States*. London: Sharpe.

Pauly, M.V. (1968) "The Economics of Moral Hazard: Comment." *American Economic Review*, 58 (5) Part 1 (June): 531–537.

Stone, D. (1993) "The Struggle for the Soul of Health Insurance." *Journal of Health Politics, Policy and Law*, 18 (2): 289–317.

Stream, C. (1999) "Health Reform in the States: A Model of State Small Group Health Insurance Market Reforms." *Political Research Quarterly*, 52 (3): 499–525.

Part I

Critical evaluation of research findings

2 What have we learned from research on small-group insurance reforms?

Kosali Ilayperuma Simon

Despite differences in estimation approaches and data sources, a growing body of evidence on the impact of health insurance reform in the small-group market paints a consistent picture. Small-group reforms have not caused havoc in the market for small-firm health insurance, but neither have these laws brought about any quantifiable benefits. Although this may seem a surprising result at first, the findings are consistent with realistic expectations about what small-group reforms could achieve.

Simply stated, the intent of small-group reform has been to enhance access by small-firm employees to affordable health insurance. While well known disparities in health insurance coverage rates exist between employees of large and small firms, eliminating or closing the gaps in coverage and premiums between large and small firms is outside the scope of what small-group reform could realistically hope to achieve. Rather, these reforms are redistributive in nature and are driven by the skewness of health care expenditure distribution. More specifically, they seek to shift some of the costs of covering high-risk employees to low-risk employees, are structured to benefit a small set of firms and employees who face difficulty obtaining health insurance, and thus have implications for the coverage rates of high- and low-risk employees in the small-group market.

While research has generally found little impact of small-group reform on the coverage of small-firm employees, some studies find evidence that certain high-risk groups have benefited at the expense of others. The literature on small-group reform has also looked at outcomes other than indicators of employee health insurance status, but there are far fewer studies in this category. Although there are interesting initial findings, the study of how regulations affect the workings of the labor market and the insurance market is still developing.

Research in small-group reform is rich in terms of the data sets and methods used, as well as the definitions of reform adopted (in terms of how particular provisions are used to characterize reform and in the definitions of reform stringency). This last feature makes a comparison of early studies challenging, since differences in results could reflect differences in how states are categorized. Fortunately, this does not appear to affect the consensus that emerges from the literature, particularly as regards insurance coverage rates.

Underlying rationale for small-group market reform

Laws commonly referred to as small-group health insurance reforms were adopted by most states in the early to mid-1990s. The aim of the legislation, as expressed in some state statutes, was to "promote the availability of health insurance coverage to small employers regardless of their health status or claims experience, to prevent abusive rating practices, and to improve the overall fairness and efficiency of the small-group health insurance market."[1] In particular, the laws were intended to solve two major problems that legislators and the general public believed plagued this insurance market.

High and volatile prices for health insurance

Small-firm health insurance is more expensive than large-firm health insurance for a variety of legitimate reasons. These include the inability of small firms to achieve economies of scale in the administration and processing of health insurance benefits (by spreading such costs over a large number of insured lives) and to avoid costs like premium taxes and benefit mandates by self-insuring using large cash reserves. In addition, small firms face increased administrative costs due to greater employee turnover and the lack of specialized human resources staff knowledgeable about health benefits. Such firms also lack the negotiating power to command lower prices. Finally, premiums available to small firms may also reflect the increased costs that insurers must incur to market health insurance products to small firms.

In addition to these valid considerations, insurers may perceive the threat of adverse selection to be greater for those small firms that seek coverage (given the generally low coverage rates among small-firm employees). As a result, small firms may face premiums that reflect such expectations and exceed those available to large firms with workers of comparable demographic characteristics. While large firms can spread costly employee medical events over a large enrollee base and thus minimize their impact on year-to-year premium changes, small firms lack such an advantage. Unfavorable claim experience in a given year can result in volatile premium experience in a subsequent period as when insurers apply durational and tier rating practices.[2]

Underwriting practices in rate setting

Health care expenditures are extremely skewed,[3] providing a strong incentive for insurers to lower their costs through favorable risk selection practices. Studies document that when small firms apply for health insurance, they are treated differently than large firms. For example, small firms have been subject to aggressive medical underwriting rules that are more common in the individual insurance market, such as subjecting employees to questionnaires and physical exams prior to writing a policy. Such underwriting procedures were used to determine whether the firm posed an acceptable risk and if not, whether it should be excluded from coverage or face higher premiums than other firms.

Small groups were also more likely to be denied coverage outright than larger firms through "red-lining" of firms and employees in particular industries and occupations viewed as high risk (McLaughlin and Zellers 1992). Small firms that received policies also faced difficulty renewing contracts if their workers recently experienced an adverse health event. In addition, small-firm employees were frequently subject to the aggressive use of pre-existing condition exclusions once a policy was offered. Such exclusions require employees with particular health conditions in a period prior to enrollment to wait a specified length of time before they can draw from their health insurance benefits.[4]

Policy instruments used

Small-group reform was expected to improve both employers' and their employees' access to health insurance by addressing the insurer practices described above. The set of provisions that I discuss are standard components of small-group reform. These include guaranteed issue, guaranteed renewal, premium rating reform, pre-existing conditions limitations, and portability provisions.

Guaranteed issue requires the insurer to accept all small firms that apply for coverage regardless of their health or claims experience. Enrollment is open either to specified plans or to all plans offered. Guaranteed renewal is a weaker form of the law that simply prevents the insurer from refusing to renew a policy. Note that both these provisions by themselves do not restrict the prices that insurers can charge in any way.

The regulations that do restrict prices are referred to as rating laws. They specify the factors on which insurers may vary rates and the extent to which they can vary. The most stringent type of rating reform is pure community rating where all groups in an insurance pool face the same premium regardless of each group's health risk. For example, small-group premiums in New York are characterized by pure community rating, with rates varying only by six geographic regions and by whether a family or single option is chosen. Modified community rating is a somewhat less stringent form of rate reform, with premiums allowed to vary according to a few health-related characteristics of the group, such as age, gender, and industry, but not by health status itself. Most states with reform have implemented premium rating bands to constrain the range of premium variation across insured groups. With this provision, premiums can only vary by a proscribed percent above and below the average premium for a particular class of insured business. Finally, rate regulations also set limits on the rate of growth in premiums from one year to the next.

Laws governing pre-existing conditions limit the time or waiting period during which an insurer can refuse to cover conditions that have been diagnosed at the start of the policy period. The waiting period is typically constrained to be six months or one year. These laws also restrict the definition of a pre-existing condition by specifying that it does not include a condition for which care was sought over a certain number of months ago. This "look-back" period is typically restricted to be six months. Portability laws, which are usually rolled into pre-existing condition provisions in discussions of reform components, allow people with continuous coverage from prior jobs to count that coverage towards the pre-existing limits on the new job. These laws also apply when an enrollee changes health plans within a small firm.

Prevalence of reform across states and over time

As noted earlier, analysts have used information on the provisions cited above to assess the prevalence of reform across states and over time and to categorize small-group reform according to its completeness and stringency. Data assembled by Simon (2000a) in Table 2.1 provide one such classification of the extent and type of regulation in the early years of reform, 1991–1996.[5]

The first category, "full reform," consists of states that passed guaranteed issue of at least two plans and any rating reform, together with the weaker renewal, portability and pre-existing conditions laws. "Partial reform" refers to states that passed rating reforms but did not guarantee the issue of health insurance. States with no issue or rating laws are called "no reform" states. Note that no states enacted guaranteed issue laws without rating reform provisions. Most states defined a small group as consisting of two to twenty-five employees in the early years, and then switched to a definition of two (and sometimes, one) to fifty employees. Some states specifically limited the rating reform provision to the smaller firm size definition while applying other laws such as the guarantee issue provisions to all firms with fewer than fifty employees. In the years after the period captured by this table, a handful of states tightened their reforms, while a few states relaxed rating reforms in reaction to the 1996 Health Insurance Portability and Accountability Act (HIPAA). Nationally, HIPAA guaranteed the issue of all plans in all states (starting July 1997), constrained the use of pre-existing condition limitations, and guaranteed health insurance portability to firms with fewer than fifty workers.[6]

Table 2.1 Timing and nature of state reforms, 1991–1996

State	*Full reform*	*Partial reform*	*Bare bones plan laws*	*State*	*Full reform*	*Partial reform*	*Bare bones plan laws*
AK	94-96			MT	94–96		92–96
AL				NC	92–96		93–96
AR		92–96	93–96	ND	95–96	92–94	92–96
AZ		94–96	92–96	NE	95–96	92–94	92–96
CA	94–96			NH	96	94–95	
CO	96	95	92–96	NJ	95–96		92–96
CT	92–96		92–96	NM	96	92–95	92–96
DC				NV			92–96
DE	94–96	92–93	94–96	NY	94–96		
FL	94–96	92–93	94–96	OH	93–96		
GA		92–96	94–96	OK	95–96	93–94	91–96
IA	93–96	92	92–96	OR		92–96	92–96
ID	94–96		96	PA			
IL		95–96	92–94	RI	93–96		91–96
IN		93–96		SC	96	92–95	
KS	93–96	92	93–96	SD	96	92–95	
KY	96		91–96	TN	94–96		94–96
LA	95–96	92–94		TX	95–96		
MA	92–96		92–96	UT		96	
MD	95–96		92–96	VA	94–96		91–96
ME	94–96	91–93		VT	93–96		
MI				WA	94–96		93–96
MN	94–96		94–96	WI		93–96	93–96
MO	95–96	94	92–96	WV		92–96	92–96
MS		96	93–96	WY	93–96		93–96

Source: Simon (2002a).

Reasonable expectations of small-group reform

Insurance companies, rather than employers, are the agents whose actions are directly constrained by small-group reform. Their responses to reform – their willingness to remain in the market, comply with reform provisions, and refrain from more subtle risk selection efforts – have implications for whether or not workers in a small firm obtain health insurance through their employer. Binding constraints on insurers regarding the plans covered by reform (e.g., bare bones plans offering limited benefits or a subset of all plans available from an insurer) and rating provisions influence the kinds of health plans that insurers are required to make available to employers as well as the permissible range of firm-specific premiums associated with such coverage. Employers, in turn, present a menu of choices to employees and their families. Responses by the latter – including new and continued participation in health insurance products made available through reform and changes in labor force participation and hours of work to qualify for such coverage – ultimately determine health insurance and labor market outcomes. To the extent that reform provisions were binding[7] and enforced,[8] these laws should have affected the two insurance market outcomes motivating reform – high and volatile health insurance premiums and insurer underwriting practices – as follows. Note that these effects follow directly from the definition of the reforms rather than rigorous theoretical treatment of the expected effects of reform that is beyond the scope of this chapter.

High and volatile premiums for health insurance

The variation in price across different small firms and the variation in price over time within a firm should decrease as a result of rating reform. However, this will depend on the type of rating reform implemented. For example, pure community rating should minimize the variation in premiums across small firms while modified community rating and rating bands permit greater variation in premiums. Such variation will depend on the number of risk adjusters in the modified community rate and the allowable deviation from the average premium proscribed by the rating bands. Year-to-year volatility in premiums may also be reduced should reform constrain the permissible rate of annual premium increases.

The effect of reform on the level of prices, however, is more complicated. Since reforms do not address underlying causes for high overall prices for small employers (e.g., failure to achieve economies of scale in administration of health benefits), they only affect the distribution at the extremes. If community-rating of premiums or tight rating bands caused the risk composition of the insurance pool to worsen by reducing premiums for poor health risks and raising premiums for good risks, while keeping the generosity of plan coverage the same, average premiums should rise. While rating reform may reduce premium variation and volatility in the small-group market, there is no reason to expect that premium differences between small and large markets will necessarily converge. Note also that any effect on prices is conditional upon guaranteed issue laws being enacted together with rate reforms. By themselves, laws restricting price are likely to be ineffective since insurers can easily work around the laws by deciding to whom they sell policies.

In theory, the combination of pure community rating laws together with guaranteed issue and renewal of health plans can cause premium levels to exacerbate over time and threaten the stability of the small-group market. For example, should low-risk enrollees defect from the market in response to the increased premiums they face under such rating and high risks increasingly dominate the market, spurred by the lower premiums they now face, premiums on average will rise. Such a market dynamic can spur successive waves of defections by lower risks, continued increases in average premiums, and ultimately, lead to a market dominated by high risks and correspondingly high premiums which may not be sustainable over time. Fortunately, research that has examined the effects of such provisions has not discerned such an adverse selection death spiral.

Premiums may be affected by provisions that limit the use of pre-existing health conditions and enhance the portability of coverage. Such provisions increase the scope of adverse risk selection by improving access to coverage for poorer health risks. Should such improved access alter the composition of the insurance pool toward poorer health risks, the average premium level under any rating scenario would increase, all else constant. Thus, opportunities for adverse selection and the reduced ability of insurers to favorably risk-select could conceivably drive premiums higher after these reforms are passed. Even absent the possibility of adverse selection, limitation of pre-existing condition clauses means that the insurance policy covers more health care costs and the price could rise for this reason too.

Underwriting practices in rate setting

The underwriting practices noted above would be mitigated if reform regulations were enforced. Denial of coverage should decline in states that adopted guaranteed issue and guaranteed renewal. But in states that have rate laws and no guaranteed issue, it is conceivable that denials would go up as insurers turned to this method of excluding potentially costly groups. Guaranteed issue laws also specify standardized benefits that make comparison easier and limit insurer ability to structure health plans to select clients by plan characteristics. Portability guarantees that movement between jobs with health insurance would become easier. Once again, any increase in benefits available to persons with pre-existing conditions should show up as a price increase, since it increases the quantity of insurance in the average policy.

Summary of empirical findings

After surveying the nature of small-group insurance reforms and the possible mechanisms by which these regulations would affect insurance market outcomes of interest, I now turn to the evidence available from five years of research on this topic. Table 2.2 provides a summary of various empirical studies conducted on small-group reform. This table identifies the key question addressed in each study (as it relates to small-group reform), the data and methods used, and the main results. One important dimension along which it is difficult to compare the results of these studies is the precise manner by which the key independent variable – the grouping of states into reform categories – is defined, since each paper tends to be unique in this respect. For example, some studies examine the impact of individual components of reform; others define reform on the basis of various combinations of reform components; while still others define reform on the basis of details of specific components of

Table 2.2 Literature review of small-group reform: summary

Key question	*Data and methods*	*Findings*
Effect of California's 1993 small-group reforms on California's small-employer offers of insurance and premiums charged to employer (Buchmueller and Jensen 1997)	*Data*. Employer surveys conducted for UC-Irvine; sample included only independent firms with three to ninety-nine employees. 715 firms in 1993 and 886 (different) firms in 1995. Comparisons are drawn with a national survey of employers from 1993 and 1995 conducted by Wayne State University *Method*. Comparison of changes in percent of California's small firms offering health insurance and change in premiums between spring 1993 and spring 1995 *Notes*. CA's reforms included PreX, rate bands, GI, GR and creation of a purchasing cooperative for small firms (HIPC)	More small firms in California offered insurance after reform than before. This is true for employers with three to nine employees and three to twenty-four employees. Ten to thirteen percentage point increase in coverage among small firms seen as possibly due to positive impact of reform Both small and large firms more likely to offer HMO/POS plans after reforms. Larger change for large employers. Managed care penetration seen as possibly causal effect of small-group laws that "leveled the playing field" for managed care insurers
Effect of New York's stringent small-group reforms on insurance coverage and type of health plan offered, relative to non-reform state (Pennsylvania) and moderate reform state (Connecticut) (Buchmueller and DiNardo 2002)	*Data*. 1988–1997 March Current Population Survey in three states, plus HIAA employer data *Method*. Difference in difference (DD) and difference-in-difference-in-difference (DDD) estimation. Control groups were workers in Pennsylvania and Connecticut, and workers in large firms in all states	New York's small-group market reforms were *not associated with decreased coverage* relative to Pennsylvania or Connecticut, states that did not have community rating laws Reforms altered structure of the small-group market, increasing managed care penetration relative to Pennsylvania and Connecticut
Effect of small-group reforms enacted in the mid-1990s on health insurance offer and enrollment rates in any plan, in an MHO, turnover in offer decisions,	*Data*. Large cross-sectional employer surveys in 1993 (NEHIS) and 1997 (RWJFEHIS). Nine states that adopted reform are compared to twelve states that did not. Small employers are defined as those with fewer than fifty	Overall, outcomes in the nine states with reforms are not very different from the non-reform states. Some states have statistically significantly different effects from the comparison groups but the pattern is not

premiums, variability in premiums and the rate of change of premiums (Marquis and Long 2001/2002)	workers *Method*. Descriptive analysis comparing outcomes in each of nine states to composite outcomes for twelve non-reform states. Differences are taken between 1993 and 1997 outcomes within a state, then compared to outcome in the non-reform states, and finally compared between small and large employers. Table shows for each state the type of rating restrictions (distinguished by age and health variation) and guaranteed issue (distinguished by none, some, and all)	consistent and thus does not suggest a causal effect of reform. Conclusion is that reforms have not brought about a downfall of the insurance market, but have also not helped small employers in terms of outcomes studied
Effect of various health insurance regulations (including small-group reform) on insurance coverage of adults (private, employer-sponsored, public) (Sloan and Conover 1998)	*Data*. 1989–1994 March Current Population Survey, persons aged 18–64 *Method*. Probit regressions. First model explains whether person has coverage. Second model explains whether that coverage is private or public. Third model explains whether private coverage is from employer or not. Fourth and fifth models explain insurance coverage among single and married workers separately. Small-group reform entered as separate variables (with some interaction by age and gender), does not group states by reform "packages" *Notes*. Regulations and policies on right-hand side include: Medicaid expansions, mandated benefits, employer tax credits, MSAs, high-risk pools, mandatory and voluntary reinsurance, purchasing alliances, GI, GR, PreX, rate limits (by health, age, gender), both individual market and small-group reforms	Only one statistically significant coefficient among all the small-group variables (eight) in the five models, suggesting reform has had no discernible effect on insurance coverage. The exception shows that community rating in small-group market *raised* the likelihood of group coverage among persons over age 55

Table 2.2 Continued

Key question	*Data and methods*	*Findings*
Effect of four categories of small-group reform: • Full reform (GI of any plan, GR, PORT, PreX + RATE) • Separately by date of first reform (early vs. recent) • Partial reform (at least one of the above, but not all) • Separately by date of first reform (early vs. recent) on, • Employer offer of insurance • Fraction of workers enrolled in health plans • Whether employer subject to "enrollee exclusion" practices (Hing and Jensen 1999)	*Data*. 1994 National Employer Health Insurance Survey (NEHIS): 17,818 private establishments employing two to fifty workers (self-insured and Hawaii excluded); 1993 coverage and worker characteristics; all small firms and separately, small firms by size category (under ten, ten to fifty) and "red-lined" small firms. Approx. 8,000 cases for coverage regression, and 7,000 cases for enrollee exclusion regression. Regulatory variables from US GAO and others *Method*. Logit and OLS regression (logit transformation) models. One year cross-sectional data, so no state fixed effects *Selected other explanatory variables*. Number of mandated benefits in state, bare-bones plan laws, county unemployment rate, HMO penetration, census region indicators	All small employers more likely to offer health insurance if reforms implemented. This applies to both full and partial reform. Laws implemented earlier have stronger effects. Bigger effect for red-lined firms Only statistically significant effects of reform on fraction enrolling in health insurance are negative, and apply only to recent partial reform Enrollee exclusion practices lower among recent full-reform states (not earlier full-reform states), and among earlier partial reform states. In one case, recent partial reform increased enrollee exclusions Owing to cross-sectional nature of data, the reported effects may capture differences among states other than their small-group reform environment
Effect of portability/PreX laws on job mobility to small firm Effect of rate restrictions (coded as 0–4 variable) on proportion of sick workers with health insurance in small firms (Kapur forthcoming)	*Data*. March CPS 1991–1997. Individuals 18–64 years. Regulatory data from US GAO and others, cross-checked for consistency *Method*. Small-firm hiring: two-step GLS procedure (to correct error terms for grouped data at the state by year level) where dependent variable is an indicator for being a new and insured worker in a small firm.	Rating reforms increase insured employment opportunities in small firms for the sick but reduce them for older workers Various alternative ways of defining the rating reform variable lead to the same conclusion Portability/PreX laws increase job mobility for insurance holders, but if without rating laws, they decrease mobility to small-firm jobs with

	Sample is limited to new hires with insurance (with large-firm insured workers forming a comparison group). Law variable interacted with cost variable Job mobility: sample is restricted to workers with insurance from their employers. Dependent variable is an indicator for being a job changer. Law variable interacted with cost variable. State fixed effects and year fixed effects are included. Small firm is defined alternatively as fewer than ten and less than twenty-five workers *Notes*. New hires and job changes are identified using the quasi-panel nature of the CPS. Family disability indicator for health measures	insurance for the sick To the extent that HIPAA bring portability laws without rate laws, this may reduce small-firm job mobility for the sick
Effects of small-group reform on probability that a worker: • Is offered health insurance • Has employment-based coverage in own or other's name Effect is evaluated for low- and high-risk groups as well as all small-firm workers (Monheit and Schone 2004)	*Data*. 1987 NMES and 1996 MEPS *Method*. DD and DDD exploiting variation in states and years adopting reform, as well as differences between small-and large-firm workers. Linear probability models. Main specification separates states into four categories based on strength of reform (also distinguishing between tight and weak rating laws). Alternative models explore definitions based on pricing and guaranteed issue alone and in combination. Predicted health expenditures are used to classify individuals as high or low risk	In the main specification, small-group reform has no statistically significant effects on any of the three outcomes In some specifications, reforms (both weak and tight rating laws) increased employer-sponsored policyholder rates for high-risk workers. In other specifications, weak reforms decrease employer-sponsored coverage rates (from all sources) for the high-risk groups. Offer rates declined in one specification for high-risk workers as a result of stringent reform

Table 2.2 Continued

Key question	*Data and methods*	*Findings*
Effect of small-group laws on employer offer of insurance. Specific laws are (entered as separate variables, and as a combination): • GI • GR • Portability • PreX limits • Bare-bones plan law (Jensen and Morrisey 1999)	*Data*. HIAA and KPMG Peat Marwick cross-sectional national surveys of employers. In total, 2,905 employers. Small firm defined as one with fewer than fifty employees. Time span: 1989–1995 *Method*. Logit model, estimated for separately for firms with under ten employees and ten to fifty employees. Analysis omitted rate reform from the specific regulation analysis to resolve multicollinearity. Small-group reform entered as six dummy variables or as one dummy for any reform. Controls for number of state-mandated benefits. No state fixed effects, although there is more than one year of data per state. Year fixed effects included	Only statistically significant effect of small-group reform is for PreX. This law increased the probability of the employer offering health insurance Effect of state-mandated benefits on firm offer decision is negative and statistically significant for small employer
Effect of small-group reforms on percentage of non-elderly in state with health insurance, and percent with private insurance (Zuckerman and Rajan 1999)	*Data*. 1990–1996 March Current Population Survey, collapsed into a state by year-level data set *Method*. OLS regression (logistic transformation of 0–100 variable) explaining the percentage of people in a state with health insurance, and the percentage with private insurance. States are grouped by reform packages. *Notes*. Outcomes is not specific to small-firm workers, thus compositional changes between small- and large-firm insurance rated within a state would not be captured. Results for	No effect of small-group reforms on insurance coverage rates at the state level

	individual market reforms show they have increased the percentage uninsured in the state	
Effect of small-group laws on probability that worker in small firm receives coverage from employer. The types of reform considered are: • Full reform (GI of at least two plans, and any rate laws) • Partial reform (no guaranteed issue, but has rate laws) • Bare bones law only (Simon 2002)	*Data*. 1992–1997 Current Population Survey (1991–1996 coverage), full-time workers aged 16–65 employed in private establishments and who worked at least thirteen weeks during the year. Sample excluded persons living in Hawaii *Method*. DDD using reform vs. non-reform states, before vs. after reform, large-group employees as a further control group *Dependent variable(s)*. Probability of employer coverage	Full-group reforms decreased coverage rates among small-firm workers, especially among low-risk (single men under age 36) workers, even when age and gender are allowed rating factors Full-group reforms increased coverage rates among some high-risk workers (e.g., married women of childbearing age with children) Constraints on rating by age and gender magnify the negative effects of other group reforms Partial reforms had statistically insignificant impact on group coverage Bare-bones laws had no impact on coverage
Effect of reform on employer probability of offering coverage, on employee probability of taking up coverage, fraction eligible for health insurance, on premium paid by firm, on employee contribution to health insurance, and on decision to offer HMO plan Definition of reform is same as above (Simon 2000a)	*Data*. 1993 National Employer Health Insurance Survey (NEHIS) and 1996 Medical Expenditure Panel Survey Insurance Component (MEPS-IC). Data exclude self-insured small groups and reflect only the largest-enrollment plan among employers that offered multiple plans *Method*. Matrix-algebra calculation of OLS coefficients and DD method comparing health insurance outcomes in small states that reformed before and after reform. (Method reflects confidentiality constraints on use of NEHIS and MEPS-IC)	Full reform increased premiums (by about 4 percent), and most of the increase was passed on to workers as increased employee contributions for coverage Full reform decreased the rate of employer coverage (by more than two percentage points), but did not decrease the rate of employer offer Full reform decreased the probability that small-group plans could exclude selected individuals or impose a PreX waiting period (by about five percentage points) Partial reform had no significant impact on offer or coverage, but was weakly associated with lower premiums and lower employee

Table 2.2 Continued

Key question	*Data and methods*	*Findings*
		contributions in high-risk firms (variously defined) No compelling evidence that regulation increased the prevalence of managed care or self-insured plans
Assesses the degree of compliance with guaranteed-issue laws by independent health insurance agents (Richardson and Hall 2000)	*Data*. Interviews collected over a period of fifteen months (1998–1999) through a series of telephonic contacts with insurance agents. Eight states with varying market rules were chosen and in each state eighteen agents were contacted *Method*. A chi-square statistic was used to test differences in responses to interviews across states. A comparison of differences among states' small-group and individual market reform laws affecting agents' willingness to offer coverage to high-risk groups and individuals was also undertaken. Further, differences in types of agent, use of public or private purchasing cooperatives and impact of laws restricting the use of genetic information were also assessed	Insurance agents highly compliant with state regulations regarding guaranteed issue Almost no difference was detected with regard to behavioral differences among types of agent (specialized independent agents, general insurance agents and/or agents referred by carriers) and the behavior seemed similar across all these professional categories
Effect of small-group reform on the probability that a small employer offered an HMO to its employees (Buchmueller and Liu 2003)	*Data*. Six separate employer surveys conducted between 1988 and 1995 (HIAA/KPMG/Peat Marwick/RWJF/KFF) yielding a total sample of 11,760 employers *Method*. Logit models where dependent	Small-group reform increased HMO penetration of the small-employer market. Stringent small-group reform leads to about a twelve percentage point increase in HMO penetration

	variable is firm's decision to offer HMO plan. A small employer is defined as one with fewer than fifty employees. State and year fixed effects are included. An interaction of small-employer indicator and reform indicator is used to capture the causal impact of reforms. Reform categories are defined by the strength of the issue and rating laws	
Effect of state-mandated health benefits and small-group reform on wages, hours and weeks of work, employment in a small firm, and prevalence of private health insurance. Reform variables are: • Number of mandated benefits, collectively and as "high-cost" categories • Small-group reform: Full reform (GI, rating, GR, PreX and portability). Partial reform (rating but no GI) (Kaestner and Simon, 2002)	*Data*. 1989–1998 Current Population Survey (1988–1997 coverage). Sample restricted to employees in small firms (with fewer than 100 workers or twenty-five workers in different specifications). Small-group laws from authors' primary research *Method*. OLS regression where dependent variables are outcomes-listed. State fixed effects, year fixed effects, plus state specific time trend included	Small-group reforms are unrelated to labor market outcomes listed. Only statistically significant effect is for health insurance Full reform associated with slight decline in employer coverage among workers in firms with fewer than twenty-five employees. Affects both part-time and full-time workers Partial reform reduces coverage among groups "vulnerable" to insurance loss: low-educated employees and young, unmarried employees without children
Effect of reforms on the individual and group health insurance structure. Specifically, effect of guaranteed issue, portability and rating reform on • Number of insurers in the market • Market shares • Herfindhal index • Share held by large insurers (Chollet *et al.* 2000)	*Data*. Data on health insurers come from the Alpha Center Health Insurer Database for 1995–1997. They span all states and District of Columbia, except Hawaii *Method*. Regression analysis, controlling for other factors such as state population. Includes state fixed effects	All else equal, guaranteed issue of all products in the small-group market resulted in more insurers selling insurance, and smaller market share for large insurers In the individual market, guaranteed issue of all products resulted in the opposite effect

reform. The studies also differ with regard to the way in which they seek to econometrically identify the impact of reform, either using reform variables in pooled cross-sectional data over several years or establishing more structured, quasi-experimental approaches that compare specific outcome measures for small-firm employees in reform states pre- and post-reform relative to a control group. Finally, some analyses study the impact of reform on the insurance coverage of the general non-elderly population while others consider the impact on groups specifically targeted by reform (e.g., small-firm employees).

Insurance coverage of small-firm workers

Health insurance coverage rates

The most frequently studied outcome in this literature is whether small-firm workers gained insurance coverage as a result of the reforms. In some papers, this outcome is specified as whether a worker in a small firm (usually defined as less than fifty workers, although less than twenty-five and less than ten workers are also used) obtains a health insurance policy from his or her employer. In other studies, the outcome is whether a small-firm worker obtains coverage from an employer or any private source. Papers that address these outcomes generally find small or no effects of reform.

In chronological order, the first published paper (Sloan and Conover 1998) looked at individuals between the ages of 18 and 64 in the March Current Population Survey (CPS) for 1989 to 1994 and examined the effect of various state health insurance regulations on whether an individual had private health insurance coverage, and if so, whether this coverage was obtained from an employer. Small-group reform was entered into the regression as variables indicating the presence and type of guaranteed issue (guaranteed access to all or just selected insurance products), the presence of guaranteed renewal, pre-existing condition waiting periods, premium rating rules (pure community rating, inability to rate based on age, and inability to rate based on sex), interacted with indicators for whether an individual is employed in a small firm. The last two rating variables are also interacted with age categories. For the empirical estimation, a law was considered to have begun a year after it was passed, and the insurance status is defined as of March of the interview year. The results generally indicate that small-group insurance has had no effect on the probability that small-firm workers have any insurance, no effect on the probability of private coverage, and no effect on the probability of employer coverage. The only statistically significant effect is the positive relationship between the inability to age-rate premiums (interacted with an indicator for being over 55 years of age) and the probability of having employer coverage. In regressions that look at the probability of being insured separately for married and single workers, none of these reform categories is statistically significant.

Zuckerman and Rajan (1999) take a different approach to testing the effects of small-group reform on insurance coverage rates also using similar data (non-elderly individuals in the March CPS from 1990 to 1996). Notable features of this study include the following: the dependent variables are the fraction of the state's non-elderly population (including children) with health insurance and the fraction with private health insurance;[9] and state regulations are entered as indicators of mutually exclusive packages of reform provisions, recognizing the high collinearity among the separate components of reform (e.g., states with tight rating restrictions often enacted stricter guaranteed issue laws). The small-group reform packages include variables for the presence of all five reform components (guaranteed issue, guaranteed renewal, rate regulation, pre-existing condition constraints, and portability), all reform components except guaranteed issue, only guaranteed issue and rate restrictions, or some other combination of reform provisions. The regression model also includes state and year fixed effects. However, these regressions do not yield separate estimates of the effect of reform on employee coverage rates in small versus large firms, nor on workers compared to nonworkers. The results show that reforms have no statistically significant impact on uninsured rates or private insurance rates at the state level. In alternative specifications, the authors enter the reform provisions separately (rather than in the combinations of provisions enacted), and also found no statistically significant effects.

Compelling evidence that small-group reforms with guaranteed issue and pure community rating did not improve health insurance coverage nor lead to an adverse selection death spiral is obtained from Buchmueller and DiNardo (2002). The authors study New York's experience with community rating (which allows premiums to vary by region and type of coverage, such as single versus family coverage) along with guaranteed issue of all plans and compare it to Connecticut, a moderate reform state with guaranteed issue of two plans (a basic and a standard plan). Connecticut also allowed premiums to vary by age, gender, industry, group size, region, and type of coverage (single versus family) and health status (the latter until 1995).[10] They also compare New York to Pennsylvania, a state that did not enact small-group reform. They use data from the 1988 to 1997 March CPS, define small firms as those with fewer than 100 workers, and restrict their samples to working adults. Buchmueller and DiNardo identify the impact of reform by examining differences in outcomes in states with and without reform, before and after reform, and across large and small firms by applying the standard "difference-in-differences-in-differences" (DDD) technique used in several studies discussed here. Outcome measures include insurance coverage rates (consisting of private coverage through any source as well as private coverage in one's own name). The authors find no statistically significant effects of reform for workers on average, nor for older workers (age was a prohibited rate factor in New York), and thus no evidence that community rating was associated with an adverse selection death spiral. An interesting finding in this paper, later explored in depth in Buchmueller and Liu (2003), is that HMO penetration in the New York small-group market appears to have increased as a result of reform.

Two other papers using the same DDD strategy but different data come to somewhat different conclusions about the effect of reform on insurance coverage rates among small-firm workers. Simon (2002) conducts a national study using the DDD technique on the March CPS from 1992 to 1997. She finds that states with both guaranteed issue of at least two plans and some rating reforms experienced a very small but statistically significant fall in insurance coverage rates among small firms (defined as those with fewer than twenty-five workers), relative to states that took on weaker restrictions. She then separates the samples into groups likely to have different expected health expenses. She finds that lower-risk individuals (e.g., single men under age 36) experienced a greater fall in insurance coverage than small-firm workers on average, and that higher-risk individuals (e.g., married women of childbearing years with children) experienced no fall in insurance coverage rates, and, in some specifications, actually appear to have increased their insurance rates.

Monheit and Schone (2004) also find an effect of reform on insurance coverage rates by employee risk status measured by expected health expenditures. Using a similar (DDD) estimation strategy, the authors use household data from the 1987 National Medical Expenditure Survey (NMES) and 1996/1997 Medical Expenditure Panel Survey (MEPS). They examine the effect of different reform packages on the following outcomes: whether the worker was offered health insurance, whether the worker had any employer-sponsored health insurance, and whether this coverage was in the worker's own name. Reforms are classified in several ways, the main distinctions being non-reform versus moderate reform (no guaranteed issue) versus stringent reform (all five reform provisions) with weak rating bands versus stringent reform with tight rating bands (including community rating). The authors find negative statistically insignificant effects for most specifications, and interpret their findings as suggestive of a negative overall effect from regulations as well as evidence that reform helped high-risk workers (in the top quarter of the expected expenditure distribution) more in states with tight rating restrictions.

Taken together, these results suggest that reforms did little to the insurance coverage rates on average. While there is some evidence that the average rates fell slightly (Simon 2002) and that the effect varied by worker risk status (Monheit and Schone 2004; Simon 2002), results from the state with the strongest reforms (New York in Buchmueller and DiNardo 2002) suggest that reforms had no effect on insurance coverage rates.

Offers of health insurance

The individual-level analysis that looked at the probability that an employee was offered health insurance (Monheit and Schone 2004) finds no statistically significant effects. All other studies cited above use the CPS, which does not contain a question about offers of health insurance in its annual March income supplement.

Most studies that examine health insurance offers to employees have used employer-level data. Jensen and Morrisey (1999) find no statistically significant effects of reform on employer decisions to offer health insurance that are likely to be causal. This study uses multiple years of data but does not employ state fixed effects. Thus it is not clear to what extent the reform variables (state-specific indicators for each of the five reform provisions) may be picking up changes due to other factors that vary at the state level. Hing and Jensen (1999) use a large employer survey, the 1993 National Employer Health Insurance Survey (NEHIS), and find that states with reforms have higher offer rates than states without reform. However, since this is a cross-sectional study, the authors cannot discern whether the states with reform are different in other ways that may increase the likelihood that an employer will offer health insurance.

Two recent studies using large employer surveys at different points in time come to the conclusion that offer rates did not change as a result of reform. Marquis and Long (2001/2002) use the 1993 NEHIS and the 1997 Robert Wood Johnson Foundation surveys and focus on nine states that had reforms effective in 1993 to 1996. Reform provisions are defined by variables separately indicating the presence of guaranteed issue, the presence of rating reforms that permitted variation by health status or by age, and for the latter, permitted a 100 percent spread between high and low premiums. Although they find some statistically significant results in their analysis, they cannot attribute causality to reform when they compare the experiences of each of the nine reform states individually to the twelve states in their survey that did not have reform. Simon (2000a) uses the 1993 NEHIS and the 1996 MEPS to examine the impact of reform on offers of coverage at the firm level using a DDD technique. The author finds that there are no statistically significant effects of reform on small-employer offers of coverage.

In summary, it appears that although states with reform may have different offer rates than states without reform, reform appears to have no causal impact on this outcome. However, the employer surveys used do not contain good measures of the health profile of the firm's employees. Since this is a key dimension along which redistribution would occur, studies that are able to find suitable data would add much to this discussion.

Health insurance premiums

Two studies exist that consider the effect of reform on premiums. Simon (2000a) uses the same technique and reform definitions as Simon (2002) on a total sample of over 30,000 firms offering health insurance in 1993 and 1996. She examines the impact of reform on the premium that is paid by the small employer, controlling for detailed information about the health plan as well as employer and some workforce characteristics. She finds that reform is associated with a statistically significant increase in premiums, but this is evident only in one specification (when states with guaranteed issue of at least two plans and rating reform are compared to all other states). When she looks at the employee contribution required for a plan, she finds a statistically significant increase in all specifications in the analysis. Marquis and Long (2001/2002) examine premium variation as well as levels for each of the nine reform states in their sample and find little impact of reform, even though individually there are some statistically significant effects. Thus, the available evidence suggests that premiums have either increased or have not been altered as a result of reform.

Labor markets

Two recent studies investigate the downstream effects that insurance reforms could have on the structure of labor markets. Kaestner and Simon (2002) study the impact of small-group insurance reform and state-mandated benefits on wages, hours of work, weeks of work, and employment in a small firm. They find no discernible impacts of reform on any of these labor market outcomes. Kapur (forthcoming) uses a refined strategy to look at the effect of specific reform components on job opportunities with health insurance in small firms for different groups of workers. She finds that rating reforms increase the employment opportunities with health insurance in small firms for those in worse health (as measured by the presence of a disability in the family) but reduce the opportunities for older workers. Portability and pre-existing conditions laws (henceforth called portability laws) accompanied by rating reform improve job mobility for those holding health insurance. But portability enacted without rating reforms has the opposite effect on the sick. Thus small-group reform may have changed worker mobility to small firms but not in ways that are all necessarily desirable. These results suggest that portability provisions in the 1996 HIPAA (unaccompanied by rating reform) may lead to reduced mobility to small firms for the sick.

Structure of the insurance market

The study of health insurers themselves is limited by the availability of information on these companies. While these agents are the ones directly regulated by the reforms, the research on small-group reforms thus far assesses their effects primarily by studying outcomes that reflect insurer behavior at the employer and worker level. Only one quantitative study to date has analyzed national insurer data (Chollet, Kirk, and Simon 2000). This study uses a limited time frame in the pre-HIPAA period (1995–1997) and thus has limited variation available to identify the effects of reform. The authors analyzed a proprietary database on insurers in all states and District of Columbia except Hawaii for a three-year period to study the effect of various components of small-group reform on the structure of the insurance market. They find that the guaranteed issue of all products seems to bring more insurers into the market, but these results are sensitive to robustness checks and thus should be treated as preliminary.

Qualitative studies on insurance market structure

The studies reviewed above are all large-scale empirical investigation of a quantitative nature. Mark Hall and colleagues have made important contributions to this literature through qualitative case studies and interviews. For example, in Richardson and Hall (2000), interviews were conducted with eighteen insurance agents for each of eight states that varied by insurance market reforms over the 1998–1999 time period. Quotations were solicited for a small business of three employees, one of whom had a chronic condition. The study found that agents are highly compliant with regulations, even when it comes to a very small group with medical problems. In only 3 percent of the calls did it appear that insurers did not follow guaranteed issue provisions.

Hall (1999) describes a more comprehensive study in which he and his colleagues closely examined markets in seven states. This research is based on interviews with regulators, insurers, agents, purchasing cooperatives, and trade groups. The market participants (insurance agents in particular) are favorable to reforms such as guaranteed issue which enable them to sell more insurance policies. While the results on premiums are difficult to interpret because of differences in the specific plan characteristics, it does appear that premiums have not changed dramatically. Managed care penetration increased in the small-group market during this time period (although the article concludes that this should not be viewed as caused by the reforms) and this may have helped keep premium increases down. The main conclusion of these qualitative studies is that while insurance reforms aim to prevent risk segmentation, they cannot be wholly successful in a market that has a high degree of price competition. Insurers may attempt to circumvent these reforms by influencing factors available to them such as giving agents higher commission for enrolling better risks.

In summary, these interviews reinforce the findings in the quantitative studies. There is some evidence that health insurance has become more accessible for those with chronic medical conditions, but the market has not produced many noticeable changes on the whole.

Conclusions

Researchers have taken a variety of approaches to discern the impact of small-group reform. Despite differences in sources of data, study methods, and definitions of reform, a consistent picture emerges showing that reforms have had almost no impact on overall insurance coverage rates. Some research also suggests that reform also had a small impact according to employee health risk, improving coverage rates for high-risk employees relative to those viewed as lower risk. However, since reform can also potentially affect other outcomes, such as changes in insurance market structure (e.g., increased market share by potentially less costly forms of coverage such as HMOs), employer decision making (such as offering health insurance), sources of coverage for employees in two-worker households, premiums, and labor market outcomes (such as wage rates and hours of work), more research in such areas is required before arriving at a comprehensive assessment of reform's impact. Finally, given that existing research does not find improvements in access to affordable health insurance for the typical small-firm worker, some understanding as to why reform has not had more of an impact on overall coverage among small-firm employees is also warranted. A comprehensive study that relates the nature of the state's reform to changes in the price of insurance paid by small firms (for a well defined insurance plan by the specific medical and demographic profile of their workers) would lead to a good understanding of what happens to premiums. This would improve our ability to conduct sound research into other downstream effects such as insurance coverage and labor market outcomes.

Small-group reforms did much statutorily to address inequities in an insurer's treatment of firms with different health-related risk profiles but did not address the fundamental reasons why health insurance costs are high, continuing to rise, and differ between small and large firms. The expectation based upon the structure of reform is that reform would negate some of the favorable selection practices used by insurers that were discussed above. However, it would be unrealistic to view small-group reform as a solution to rising insurance prices and falling coverage rates among small firms.

Beyond the study of actual outcomes, our understanding of the potential value of reform would also benefit from a systematic assessment of the welfare implications of the redistribution implicit in the regulations. If reform leads to less insurance coverage for low-risk individuals (because they drop coverage or obtain less generous coverage when the composition of the risk pool changes and premiums rise), but helps a few high-risk uninsured (or low-insured) individuals gain coverage, is society better off?

More generally, is employer-based health insurance the optimal way to insure high-risk individuals (especially those in small firms) and can small-group reform ever adequately address the financial concerns of insurers regarding adverse selection? Or are there other options to consider, such as expansions of existing federal government programs for employees and family members who are high risk (as was done under Medicare for persons with end-stage renal disease) and state-sanctioned high-risk pools, which would expand coverage to poor health risks without jeopardizing the coverage of those in better health? Consideration of these issues and additional research on the direct and indirect effects of reform can help to illuminate the full benefits and costs of small-group market reform.

Notes

1 Section 2 of the 1992 National Association of Insurance Commissioners (NAIC) Small Employer Health Insurance Availability Model Act.

2 Hall (1992, 1994). Under tier rating, small groups are classified according to their members' health risks and claims experience and can be moved to a higher rating tier when adverse medical events occur. Under durational rating, small groups initially obtain low premiums but can be subject to subsequent large premium increases as insurer gains from medical screening and pre-existing condition limitations are reduced.

3 The top 1 percent accounts for 30 percent of all health spending. Least expensive 50 percent accounts for only 3 percent of spending (Berk and Monheit 1992).

4 Other than insurance market-related issues discussed above, another reason why health insurance outcomes in small firms may be different from those in large firms is that large firms tend to differ from small firms systematically in many aspects such as industry, profit margins, and pay (Brown *et al.*, 1990).

5 For other examples of reform classifications see Sloan and Conover (1998), table 1, and table 1 of Marquis and Long (2001/2002).

6 HIPAA (Public Law 104–191 of 1996) can essentially be thought of as three separate pieces of legislation. One is related to insurance reform (Title I), while the second concerns administrative simplifications, preventing fraud and abuse and medical liability reform (Title II). The third (Title III) concerns tax-related reforms, such as the provision for Medical Savings Accounts. The most relevant part of HIPAA for this discussion is the guaranteed issue of all provisions in Section 2711 of PL 104–191 of 1996. For more details of how HIPAA affects small employers with fewer than fifty employees, see http://www.cms.gov/hipaa/hipaa1/content/qa-emp.asp (access date September 2003). For the complete text of HIPAA, see http://www.cms.gov/hipaa/hipaa1/content/HIPAASTA.pdf (access date September 2003).

7 This would mean that the conditions called for in the statutes weren't already *de facto* industry norms. For example, there is evidence that many mandated benefits laws mandated benefits that were already being covered by almost all insurance policies sold (Gruber 1994).

8 This also assumes an accurate understanding of the requirements between the insurance industry and the regulators (thus no need for clarification of rules).

9 In a study where the key independent variable changes at the state by year level, standard errors are miscalculated in an ordinary least squares regression if the unit of observation is the individual. There are several techniques that

researchers use to correct this problem. One is to cluster the standard errors at the level at which the independent variable varies (state by year), or else to include fixed effects (state by year). Another way to counter this problem is to create the dependent variable also at the same level (by state by year), which is the approach used here.

10 Note that in Connecticut these provisions applied only to firms with fewer than twenty-five workers while in New York these provisions applied to all firms with fewer than fifty workers. Thus, the definition of a small firm as one with fewer than 100 workers is more appropriate in the case of New York than in the case of Connecticut.

References

Berk, M. and Monheit, A. (1992) "The Concentration of Health Expenditures: An Update." *Health Affairs*, 11: 145–149.

Brown, C., Hamilton, J., and Medoff, J. (1990) *Employers Large and Small*. Cambridge, MA: Harvard University Press.

Buchmueller, T.C. and DiNardo, J. (2002) "Did Community Rating Induce an Adverse Selection Death Spiral? Evidence from New York, Pennsylvania, and Connecticut." *American Economic Review*, 92 (1): 280–294.

Buchmueller, T.C. and Jensen, G.A. (1997) "Small Group Reform in a Competitive Managed Care Market: The Case of California, 1993–1995." *Inquiry*, 34: 249–263.

Buchmueller, T.C. and Liu, S. (2003) "Small Group Reform and HMO Penetration in the Small Group Market." Working paper, University of California, Irvine.

Chollet, D., Kirk, A., and Simon, K. (2000) "The Impact of Access Regulation on Health Insurance Market Structure." Report to Assistant Secretary for Planning and Evaluation (ASPE), http://aspe.hhs.gov/health/reports/impact/.

Gruber, J. (1994) "State-mandated Benefits and Employer-provided Health Insurance." *Journal of Public Economics*, 55 (3): 433–464.

Hall, M.A. (1992) "The Political Economics of Health Insurance Market Reform." *Health Affairs*, 11: 108–124.

Hall, M.A. (1994) *Reforming Private Health Insurance*. Washington, DC: AEI Press.

Hall, M.A. (1999) "The Competitive Impact of Small Group Health Insurance Reform Laws." *University of Michigan Journal of Law Reform*, 32 (4): 685–726.

Hing, E. and Jensen, G.A. (1999) "Health Insurance Portability and Accountability Act of 1996: Lessons from the States." *Medical Care*, 37 (7): 692–706.

Jensen, G.A. and Morrisey, M.A. (1999) "Small Group Reform and Insurance Provision by Small Firms, 1989–1995." *Inquiry*, 36 (2): 176–187.

Kaestner, R. and Simon, K.I. (2002) "Labor Market Consequences of State Health Insurance Regulation." *Industrial and Labor Relations Review*, 56 (1): 136–159.

Kapur, K. (forthcoming) "Labor Market Implications of State Small Group Health Insurance Reform." *Public Finance Review*.

Marquis, M.S. and Long, S. (2001/2002) "Effects of 'Second Generation' Small Group Health Insurance Market Reforms, 1993–1997." *Inquiry*, 38: 365–380.

Monheit, A.C. and Schone, B. (2004) "How has Small Group Market Reform Affected Employee Health Insurance Coverage?" *Journal of Public Economics*, 88 (1–2): 237–254.

National Association of Insurance Commissioners (1998) *Model Laws and Regulations*. Kansas City, MO: NAIC.
Richardson, C. and Hall, M.A. (2000) "Agents' Behavior under Health Insurance Market Reform." *Journal of Insurance Regulation*, 18 (3): 341–356.
Simon, K.I. (2000a) "The Impact of Small Group Health Insurance Reform on the Price and Availability of Health Benefits." Unpublished MS.
Simon, K.I. (2000b) "Legislative Summaries of State Small Group Health Insurance Reforms 1990–1999." Unpublished manuscript.
Simon, K.I. (2002) "Did Small Group Health Insurance Reforms Work?" Unpublished MS.
Sloan, F.A. and Conover, C.J. (1998) "Effects of State Reforms on Health Insurance Coverage of Adults." *Inquiry*, 35: 280–293.
Zellers, W., McLaughlin, C., and Frick, K.D. (1992) "Small-business Health Insurance: Only the Healthy Need Apply." *Health Affairs*, 11 (1): 174–178.
Zuckerman, S. and Rajan, S. (1999) "An Alternative Approach to Measuring the Effects of Insurance Market Reforms." *Inquiry*, 36: 44–56.

3 What have we learned from research on individual market reform?

Deborah Chollet

Despite its small size, the individual health insurance market plays an important role in a voluntary, private–public "system" of health insurance. At least in principle, it accommodates the population without access to either an employer plan or a public program. These include primarily workers and their families, but also a significant proportion of self-employed individuals, retirees, and dependents.

Prices in the individual health insurance market are notoriously high. The administrative cost of individual coverage as a percentage of premium is much higher than in the group market, sometimes accounting for nearly half of the premium. Unless restricted by state law, insurers may deny or aggressively limit coverage, and they may vary premiums (by many orders of magnitude) for differences in age, gender, occupation, location, and past or present health status at the time of issue. In at least six states[1] and the District of Columbia, insurers may further adjust premiums as health status changes. The federal HIPAA that reformed group coverage did very little to assist people who buy coverage in the individual market, and it did even less for those who "live" in the individual market – those without recent access to employer coverage.

The small size of the individual market makes it relatively volatile. Changes in insured lives and premium volume that would be minor in the group market can represent a major change against the much smaller base of business in the individual market and (because most individual insurers write very little premium volume) can profoundly affect any given insurer's business. But ironically, because the individual health insurance market is a residual market, it is peculiarly subject to change: growth in employer coverage especially can take significant business from the individual market (and it may take disproportionately its preferred risks – younger workers who most benefit from expanding group coverage), while economic recession may fail to restore lives to the more costly individual market.

These problems of the current market notwithstanding, the individual market is a very appealing platform for expanding health insurance coverage, in that it avoids many of the difficulties that strategies tied to employer coverage encounter. Expansion of individual coverage – for example, via refundable tax credits – could avoid burdening small employers (where most uninsured adults work), facilitate targeted subsidies to low-income and/or high-risk individuals, and stabilize coverage for highly mobile workers and their dependents. However, many analysts familiar with the individual market recommend that substantial change – and greater uniformity – be brought to the individual market before policymakers presume that it is adequate to support expanded health insurance coverage. If HIPAA is a model for developing greater uniformity nationwide, each state might be called upon to enact reforms under federal guidelines to produce greater uniformity in the ways that individual insurance products are issued and priced.

The individual health insurance market is unique in a number of ways that affect the impact of regulations to improve access or affordability. Therefore, I first summarize studies that describe the market as context for understanding the findings of the studies that have evaluated the impacts of reform. The discussion is organized as follows. I begin by reviewing the size and characteristics of the population that buys individual health insurance. Next, I describe the supply-side structure of the market, focusing on differences at the state level. I briefly review what is known about the demand for insurance, summarize evidence about biased selection in this market, and discuss insurers' underwriting practices that have been used to address the potential for adverse selection. Finally, I consider state access regulation intended to curb insurer underwriting and promote access to individual coverage and provide concluding remarks.

Consumers of individual coverage

Consumers without access to group coverage or public programs comprise the market for individual coverage. Thus, as a residual market, it is small. Of the estimates available from population surveys, the Current Population Survey (CPS) typically produces the highest estimates of the number and percent of the population with individual coverage: in 2001, an estimated 16.4 million Americans under age 65 reported having individual coverage at some time during the year.[2] This is less than 7 percent of the non-elderly population, and equal to about 9 percent of those who reported having private health insurance of any kind during the year.

Reflecting problems of access and high price in the individual market, persons without group or public coverage are much more likely – in fact, two and a half times as likely in 2001 – to be uninsured (16.5 percent) as to be insured in the individual market (6.6 percent). Just 15 percent of the population who were neither insured in an employer plan nor enrolled in a public program during the year bought individual coverage.

Although interpretation of CPS data over time is complicated by changes in the survey questions and field administration, it is the only source of information about long-term trends in coverage (Fronstin 2003). CPS estimates suggest that the number of persons with individual coverage has generally declined since 1993, when 17.5 million persons reported individual coverage. Although data adequate to estimate the determinants of change in individual health insurance purchases are lacking, it appears that at least some of the decline in individual coverage between 1993 and 2000 (from 7.7 percent of the non-elderly population to 6.6 percent) was associated with growth in employer-based coverage (which rose from 64.3 percent of the non-elderly population to more than 67 percent). Conversely, as employer coverage declined by 2.1 percentage points between 2000 and 2001 (to 65.6 percent of the non-elderly population), the purchase of individual coverage grew by 1.2 percentage points – compensating for about half of the loss of group coverage.

Historically, the population that buys individual health insurance is much like the general population under age 65. Most are adults under age 45, or children younger than age 18. Most live in families headed by a full-time full-year worker, and are wage or salaried workers (not self-employed). Most live in families with income above 300 percent of poverty, and most live in metropolitan areas (Chollet 2001).

However, the individually insured population is more diverse than the employer-insured population. In general they are older; they are more likely to be low-income; they are more likely to live in rural areas; and they are more likely to live in a family headed by a part-time or part-year worker, a nonworker, or a self-employed worker. Published data from the 1997 National Survey of America's Families (NSAF) indicate that the vast majority of individually insured workers (about 81 percent) are employed in firms with fewer than 100 employees. By comparison, just half of workers with employer coverage were employed in such firms (Haley and Zuckerman 2000).

The supply of individual insurance: market structure

In all states, many fewer insurers write individual coverage than write group coverage. In part, this reflects the much lower demand for individual coverage and the low premium volume insurers can expect in this market. But it also reflects the historical dominance of Blue Cross and Blue Shield (BCBS) plans in the individual market and the reluctance of some insurers (in particular, HMOs) to compete in the individual market where smaller commercial insurers typically underwrite very aggressively. Counting insurers by the number of states in which they sold individual health insurance products, 643 insurers wrote coverage in the individual market in 2001, compared to 2,151 insurers that wrote group coverage (Chollet *et al.* 2003).

While the individual market in every state has fewer insurers than the group market (including BCBS plans, commercial insurers, and HMOs), it has many more insurers relative to premium volume. In 2001, total earned premium volume in the group insurance market was nearly fourteen times that of insurers in the individual market, but the group market had just 3.3 times as many insurers (Chollet *et al.* 2003).[3]

In nearly all states, the individual market is very concentrated: in 2001, just three insurers held at least two-thirds of the market in all but three states (Colorado, Florida, and Wisconsin). BCBS plans dominated the individual market, holding 57 percent of the market nationally and more than 90 percent of the market in five states (Alaska, Arkansas, Kentucky, Ohio, and Rhode Island). HMOs dominated the individual market only in Utah (where they held 57 percent of the market) and the District of Columbia (where they held 51 percent).[4]

It is unclear whether state reforms to improve access or affordability may increase market concentration, as marginal carriers leave and larger insurers pursue greater market share. In general, constraints on underwriting and pricing encourage insurers to gain market share to withstand cost shocks that they are forbidden to screen out (guaranteed issue), price out (rate constraints), or shed at renewal (guaranteed renewal). However, this impact can be substantially muted if insurers use other available strategies to stratify risk.[5]

Because the market is highly skewed, the vast majority of insurers in the individual market survive on very little premium volume in any one state. Very low average premium volume contributes both to the volatility of individual insurers' underwriting losses and to the high share of premiums devoted to administrative costs. While data measuring the margin between premiums earned and medical claims paid have been unavailable historically, it is commonly presumed to range as high as 40 percent (Pauly and Nichols 2002). However, the margin appears to vary widely, both among insurers by premium volume (with the smallest insurers often running underwriting losses) and among states that regulate individual premiums.[6]

Consumer demand for individual coverage

Only one study has attempted to estimate the price elasticity of demand for individual coverage.[7] Considering the demand for individual health insurance among workers without access to employer coverage in 1988, Marquis and Long (1995) concluded that demand is inelastic with respect to price (−0.3 to −0.4) and even more inelastic with respect to income (0.15). Various methodological problems with this study suggest that consumer demand may vary more with income and price than such estimates indicate.[8] However, such inelastic demand suggests that reform efforts to reduce premiums to lower-income populations, in particular, may not elicit a large increase in coverage.

The difficulty of measuring supply in the individual market complicates the measurement of demand. As a result, simply observing who buys insurance and at what price (as Marquis and Long did) without accounting for the supply side of the market may offer little information about true demand elasticity. Historically, insurers have responded to strong consumer preferences for more comprehensive insurance products (over "bare bones" products), differentiating them with complex cost-sharing provisions, specific and general exclusions, and internal limits on coverage to constrain price. This has produced substantial variation in the actuarial value of policies, but the combined premium and out-of-pocket cost of individual coverage has remained high, eliminating many consumers from the market on the basis of income alone (Young and Wildesmith 2002; Gabel *et al.* 2002).[9] Among consumers who remain, the downside risks of attempting to change policies limit their practical opportunities to demonstrate income and price elasticity: by changing policies or carriers, consumers may expose themselves to new underwriting and significant unintended costs (for example, loss of their accustomed providers). These "cliffs" in supply, unless adequately measured, may be construed as price- and income-inelastic demand.

Biased selection

The individual market is believed to be much more susceptible to adverse selection than the group market for the usual reason of asymmetric information between sellers and buyers of insurance. Because individual coverage is typically very expensive, the incentive to buy health insurance only when one anticipates needing health care is presumed to be very strong. Expecting adverse selection, insurers underwrite aggressively in this market, denying applicants, excluding coverage for specific conditions or entire body systems, and varying price to reflect past or present health problems. Some individual market reforms – guaranteed issue and renewal, and constraints on pre-existing condition exclusions – are intended to reduce or eliminate this kind of insurer behavior.

However, researchers observing the individual market have been unable to confirm that market-wide adverse selection in fact occurs. Pauly and Percy (2000) concluded that the population with individual coverage is healthier than the general population. Using different population survey data, both Vistnes and Monheit (1997) and Brennan (2000) concluded that they are approximately as healthy as the population with employer coverage.[10] Similarly, Swartz and Garnick (1999) were unable to find adverse selection in New Jersey's individual insurance market, even after the state prohibited insurer underwriting and implemented pure community rating. They found that the enrolled population in New Jersey's individual market (without insurer underwriting) was healthier than the population that did not enroll, possibly because income and health status generally are correlated.

While differences between the health status of the individually insured population and the general population may reflect insurers' success in medical underwriting (as Pauly and Percy suggest), the Vistnes–Monheit study suggests that insurers are ultimately no more successful in capturing a healthy pool of enrollees in the individual market (where insurer underwriting is notorious) than in the group market (where employers and insurers have had much less freedom to underwrite health risk even before HIPAA).[11] The Swartz–Garnick study implies that self-selection may occur in the individual market, even if insurer underwriting is substantially eliminated: many individuals who anticipate significant expenditures for health care may be unable to pay high premiums, or unwilling to pay them if they also expect to pay high cost sharing when insured.

While the results of these studies are intriguing, a word of caution to policymakers is in order. All of these studies rely on simple observation of the health characteristics of the insured population. This method is likely to reveal only the most extreme adverse selection. As importantly, their findings may fail to comport with many insurers' actual experience for at least two reasons.

First, the impact of underwriting deteriorates over time, so that underwritten populations as a whole gradually come to resemble populations that are not underwritten. Indeed, various researchers have observed that many people with costly and chronic conditions (prior or ongoing at the time they are surveyed) have individual insurance. However, because most states prohibit re-underwriting at renewal, their premiums may be close to average (Pauly and Herring 1999; Pauly and Nichols 2002). While turnover in the individual market is presumed to be high,[12] survey data offer no reliable measures of the proportion of the insured population who recently entered the individual market or changed policies. Thus, while newly underwritten consumers may in fact be much healthier than those insured in the individual market longer-term, the insured population considered as a whole may look like populations that were not underwritten at all.

Second, many individual insurers may experience adverse selection – and even deliberately engineer adverse selection – while others are able to avoid it. Thus some (possibly most) insurers' complaints about adverse selection may be valid, but adverse selection may not occur market-wide. Insurers that attempt to engineer biased selection in some products presumably do so to maximize profit or revenue margins across all of their business, accepting short-term losses in selected products. These practices can drive prices very high for individuals with health problems, even when state regulation limits price variation for health status within products:

- Chollet and Kirk (1998) observed some large carriers routinely denied enrollment in their managed care option to applicants with health problems, instead steering them to the carrier's fee-for-service option.
- Insurers may carry "closed" blocks of business in which prices

typically spiral upward (US GAO 1997). Defined as plans in which the insurer is no longer accepting new enrollment, closed plans may escalate premiums not only because enrollees become older, but also as they remain in the plan longer and rising premiums drive out lower-risk enrollees.[13] Insurers may expedite this spiral by raiding their own closed block, selectively offering enrollees in their closed block entry into another of their plans.

- In states that require insurers to sell a "basic and standard" insurance option (intended to help consumers comparison-shop for insurance) but also allow insurers to sell other similar products, it is generally presumed that insurers try to use the standard product as a "dumping ground" for high-risk consumers, driving up its price. While this presumption is widely held, however, careful research either supporting or refuting it is scarce.[14]

Insurer underwriting

In forty-five states and the District of Columbia, insurers may deny coverage to applicants based on their assessment of whether the applicant is likely to be a high user of health care. In twenty-one states, insurers may deny all products to any applicant at any time (Pollitz and Sorian 2002). Alternatively (and unless precluded by state law), insurers may issue individual policies but exclude coverage for specific conditions or whole body systems, and they may "rate up" individual premiums to reflect the insurer's perception of greater risk. These practices in the individual market sharply contrast with the practices that they are held to by federal law (HIPAA) in the group market, where insurers cannot deny coverage to a group, nor exclude or rate coverage within a group owing to health status.

Comprehensive measures of the extent to which insurers underwrite in the individual market are unavailable. However, the literature offers consistent evidence that it is aggressive and extensive, where insurance regulation permits:

- In a report to Congress describing health insurance markets in seven states, the US General Accounting Office (US GAO 1997) reported denial rates by large carriers that ranged as high as 33 percent (reported by a carrier in Illinois over its national book of business).
- In a survey of ten states' individual insurance markets in 1998, based on a stratified sample of insurers in each state, Chollet and Kirk (1998) observed typical "rate-ups" for health status that ranged from 75 percent to 200 percent. In most states (where individual coverage is not guaranteed issue), insurers themselves constrained rate differences by denying coverage to individuals with the most costly health problems or by issuing exclusion riders.[15]

- Pollitz *et al.* (2001) attempted to obtain offers of conventional coverage from nineteen insurers in eight insurance markets for seven hypothetical individuals with health problems that ranged from simple seasonal hay fever to HIV, submitting sixty applications for coverage for each individual. Only 10 percent of applications obtained "clean offers" at standard rates with no restrictions on coverage. However, 37 percent of applications were denied, 28 percent were offered substandard coverage, 13 percent were rated up, and 12 percent were offered substandard coverage and also rated up. The probability of denial, substandard offer, and rate-up varied widely both by the applicants' specific condition, and for each applicant across markets.
- Considering coverage among a sample of adults with chronic conditions in two communities in Indiana, Stroupe *et al.* (2000) concluded that chronically ill individuals, when they are insured, are systematically underinsured. This study attributed the significantly lower level of coverage reported by individuals with chronic conditions to permanent exclusion riders.

The literature also suggests that enforcement of underwriting constraints in some states may be a problem. In two of fifteen states with rating constraints in statute in 1999, insurance regulators did not actively review insurer rates (Kirk and Chollet 2002).

The effect of access reforms on markets and coverage

Federal law governing individual health insurance markets is very limited. HIPAA requires an avenue of access into the individual health insurance market for "eligible" individuals – people who have had at least eighteen months of continuous coverage without a significant break, are leaving group coverage, have exhausted available COBRA benefits, and meet other requirements.[16] HIPAA also requires guaranteed renewal in the individual market. But unlike its provisions in the group market, HIPAA does not restrict insurers in the individual market from imposing pre-existing exclusions (either look-back or waiting periods), nor does it require individual-to-individual portability or restrict insurers' rating practices.[17]

While many states have enacted requirements that meet or exceed HIPAA's provisions to improve access to coverage in the individual market (Chollet, Kirk, and Simon 2000),[18] HIPAA itself prompted little change: just four states enacted broader guaranteed issue protections than they had in place previously,[19] and just twelve enacted provisions as broad as HIPAA's federal fallback standard (all products guaranteed issue). Absent limits on rating, insurers can and have used premium rate-ups to deter access even to HIPAA-eligibles (Pollitz *et al.* 2000).[20] In fact, many states have enacted some form of guaranteed issue without rating limits,[21] and others have enacted rating limits without guaranteed issue.[22]

A number of empirical studies have attempted to evaluate the impacts of access reforms in health insurance markets, although most have focused on small-group reforms and markets (see Chapter 2). The earliest study that explicitly addressed individual coverage (Zuckerman and Rajan 1999) estimated the concurrent impact of small-group and individual health insurance reforms on the statewide rates of no coverage and private (combined group and individual) coverage, respectively, in 1994. This study concluded that individual-market guaranteed issue raised the rate of uninsured overall.[23] Similarly, restrictions on pre-existing condition exclusions (measured as a simple dummy variable) increased uninsured rates (significant with 90 percent confidence), and decreased the rate of private insurance coverage (significant with 99 percent confidence).

Only a few studies looking for impacts of insurance market reforms have focused directly on the individual market:

- Chollet, Kirk, and Simon (2000) evaluated the impact of individual insurance market reforms with respect to measures of supply in the individual market between 1995 and 1997. Unlike earlier work, this study constructed continuous variables for restrictions on pre-existing condition exclusions and rating restrictions, and differentiated all-product guaranteed issue from some-product guaranteed issue. The study found that guaranteed issue of all products increased market concentration in the state (measured as the market share of the largest five insurers) and restrictions on health rating both increased market concentration (measured by the Herfendahl index) and reduced commercial insurers' market share.[24] However, ongoing research by Chollet and Mays (2002) has failed to find any relationship between access regulation of any kind and insurers' propensity to withdraw from markets. Only one variable – active state review of insurance rates (regardless of whether rates were actually regulated) – may have affected insurers' decision to exit the market.
- Chollet, Simon, and Kirk (2000) estimated the effect of various access regulations on the probability of individual coverage among persons aged 18–64 during 1995–1997, conditional on their having neither employer nor public coverage. Again using continuous variables to measure rate regulation and constraints on pre-existing exclusions, this study (like Zuckerman and Rajan) concluded that guaranteed issue of all products reduced the probability of individual coverage (by nearly eleven percentage points), although guaranteed issue of some products did not. Neither rate bands (on either health or age) nor other forms of regulation (including pre-existing condition exclusions) had a significant effect on coverage.[25]
- Swartz and Garnick (1999) examined whether implementation of the New Jersey Individual Health Coverage Program (IHCP), a reform effort that included guaranteed issue and pure community rating, led

to adverse selection in the individual insurance market, but found no early evidence change. Work by Monheit *et al.* (2004) has found that new enrollees to the IHCP appear to be significantly older than earlier enrollees, suggesting that the IHCP may be retaining adverse health risks, but it is unclear whether this is a result of reform.[26]

- Chollet and Schone (2002) considered the impact of high-risk pools on individual coverage, controlling for other market regulation. This study considered both the probability of individual coverage among adults aged 18–64 in a later period (1997–1999) and the health status of covered individuals. It concluded that larger high-risk pools improve the odds of coverage among lower-income healthy adults (below 300 percent of poverty). However, in nearly all states high-risk pools are too small to have any discernible effect: they do not increase coverage among either higher-income adults or adults with health problems. Unlike earlier work, this study concluded that neither guaranteed issue nor the prohibition of exclusion riders affected coverage. However, rate regulation (controlling for the presence and size of a high-risk pool) had complex effects. Narrower rate bands on health raised coverage among some (lower-income healthy adults and among adults with health problems), but narrower comprehensive rate bands reduced coverage among healthy adults, and among low-income healthy adults in particular. The finding that more restrictive comprehensive rate bands reduce coverage among healthy adults suggests that average premiums may have increased for better risks, having the unintended effect of driving them from the market.

In summary, the literature evaluating the impact of regulation in the individual market on either the supply characteristics of the market or coverage is new and limited by a number of important problems. Differences in the measurement of regulatory variables have strongly affected the studies' varied empirical results. Nearly all studies have relied on the same basic data – various years of the March Current Population Survey – that have known problems in the measurement of health insurance coverage. Finally, each study of this market has relied on both early experience with market regulation (just as states initiated change) and very few observations of change.

Very few states have enacted additional reforms of their individual market since 1997, although some subsequently have modified or repealed their reform legislation. The slow pace of further regulatory change in this market may impede the pace of empirical analysis of regulatory impacts, although there clearly is opportunity for analysis of alternative population-level data (should survey data with sufficient sample size become available) and analysis of longer-term adjustments that may follow regulatory change.

There also is ample opportunity for further qualitative analysis of regulatory impacts, if they are soundly structured evaluations with valid control groups. Following the states' reforms in the 1990s, a number of qualitative studies emerged describing the experience of New Jersey (Swartz and Garnick 2000), New York (Chollet and Paul 1994; Hall 2000a), Vermont (Hall 2000b), and Washington, Kentucky, and Massachusetts (Kirk 2000). However, it is difficult to glean many general rules or lessons from this research: the reforms differed widely, as did their acceptance by insurers or other interests and their paths of implementation; and all were process studies, as opposed to a formal evaluation of outcomes. Nevertheless, some general observations emerge:

- No state that implemented reform is sure of its impacts on coverage. In all states, employer coverage grew with improving labor markets, and individual coverage declined – irrespective of reforms.
- No state is sure of the impact of its reforms on the supply of health insurance products. Some states prohibited the sale of pure indemnity products in their individual markets, but others that did not (e.g., Massachusetts and New York) have seen their individual markets convert strongly or entirely to managed care – either HMO or POS.
- No state is sure of the impact of reform on market structure. Many reform states had commercial insurers (with characteristically low premium volume and little market share) close their individual products and ultimately leave the individual market. But others (e.g., Massachusetts) had new commercial insurers enter their market and succeed following reform.

If one overarching lesson about state reform emerges from these states' experiences, it is political – and salient to both policymakers and researchers: states that have insufficient information to evaluate the condition of their market (e.g., Kentucky and Washington) are unlikely to maintain reforms against the rhetoric of insurers that oppose them.

Finally, while no state observed either lower insurance premiums or greater individual coverage following reform, either would have been an unrealistic expectation. In an environment of major change, insurers are likely to price conservatively, and in fact may intentionally set prices high to slow new enrollment. No premium data are available to detect whether reform states saw systematically different premium increases than other states. And even in states with reliable information about covered lives or population, the growth of group coverage over the mid and late 1990s confounded the states' attempts to evaluate their own reforms (Chollet 2001).

Conclusions

In large part because the individual market is small, it is idiosyncratic. Its small size contributes to volatility: virtually no change in this market can be regarded as marginal. The concentration of supply, with the vast majority of insurers in every state surviving on extremely low premium volume, contributes to insurers' perceptions of adverse selection. The diversity of consumers in this market (they are both older and lower-income than group-insured lives) and their much higher lapse rates put small insurers individually at great risk of adverse selection, even if adverse selection does not occur market-wide. Thus, insurers are inclined to underwrite aggressively and to subvert federal and state laws that are intended to curb underwriting. And while insurers are reluctant to abandon practices they see as potential survival tactics, consumers are reluctant to enter the market at all – individuals without group or public coverage are nearly three times as likely to be uninsured as to buy individual coverage.

The research literature, while generally meager, offers some broad lessons for policymakers in crafting rules for the individual market. These are as follows:

- While many – arguably most – consumers are eliminated from the individual market on the basis of income alone, those who do buy individual coverage appear to have inelastic demand for coverage. Therefore, initiatives that achieve only modest reductions in price – or modest growth in household income – are likely to produce no significant gain in coverage.
- There is little evidence that the individual market, as a whole, has problems of adverse selection. However, there is some evidence that (1) the experience of specific insurers may differ substantially from aggregate market experience; and (2) changes in group coverage may produce biased exit of consumers from the individual market. In markets that support a large number of very small insurers, these insurers' experience may vary widely, and perceptions of adverse selection market-wide may be exaggerated.
- When unconstrained by state regulation, insurer underwriting is very aggressive. Even in states that limit underwriting at issue or renewal, insurers may use an array of strategies – such as closing blocks of business – in an attempt to keep their business freshly underwritten.
- The literature is inconsistent with respect to the impact of access reforms on coverage. While early studies indicated that guaranteed issue reduces individual coverage (presumably because insurers raise premiums to accommodate the entry of bad risk), more recent studies found no evidence that either guaranteed issue or renewal affects the probability of coverage or biases enrollment in the individual market as a whole.
- Rate regulation – establishing specific or comprehensive rate bands – may affect coverage. Specifically, community rating (prohibiting use of health status as a rate factor) may increase coverage among individuals with health problems without discouraging coverage among

the population as a whole. However, comprehensive rate bands (in the limit, pure community rating) may drive average premiums higher and discourage coverage among adults who otherwise are uninsured.

- Finally, it is unclear whether regulation encourages the growing concentration of supply in state markets. Specifically, states with guaranteed issue of all products appear to have more concentrated markets, with the largest insurers holding greater market share. However, insurers do not appear more likely to either exit or merge when the state implements guaranteed issue or rate regulation. However, small insurers may be more inclined to exit states that actively review rate changes, even if they do not actually regulate rates. In all states such insurers, individually and collectively, hold very little market share.

Notes

1 Hawaii, Idaho, Illinois, Kentucky, Ohio, and Wyoming. Various other states allow insurers to reunderwrite some policies (Pollitz 2003).

2 Both the Medical Expenditure Panel Survey (MEPS) and the National Survey of America's Families (NSAF) produce smaller estimates of this population than the CPS: approximately 11 million to 12 million persons – just 5 percent of the population under age 65. Differences in the surveys' questions, administration and sample designs all drive the differences in these estimates, as may small differences in how researchers have defined the reference population for published estimates (e.g., including or excluding members of the military and their families).

One reason for differences in estimates of individual coverage may be the inconsistent allocation of individuals to association coverage. For example, individual coverage obtained through an association marketed at workplaces (e.g., to employees of automobile retail dealerships) may be reported as employer coverage. Others may report the same coverage as individual coverage. Because population surveys do not ask specifically about association coverage and insurers are not required (on the standard reporting form) to distinguish association business from other group business, there are no reliable estimates of the proportion of group coverage that is association business.

3 Specifically, insurers in the individual market reported average earned premiums of $11.9 million (per insurer), while group insurers averaged $59 million in earned premiums.

4 Nevertheless, HMOs grew especially fast in the individual market during the mid-1990s, as some states began to require that HMOs write individual coverage. Between 1995 and 1997, HMO market share climbed nearly ten points in the individual market, compared to less just three points in the group market (Chollet, Kirk, and Chow 2000). However, by 2001, HMOs had dropped to from 26 percent to just 20 percent of the individual market, losing ground in large states (California and New York) where they had dominated in 1997 (Chollet *et al.* 2003).

5 Where allowed, carriers often use tiered or durational rating, or close blocks of business. In effect, these strategies serve to underwrite policyholders on an ongoing basis.

6 High administrative costs may be more prevalent in states that do not actively review rates in the individual market, although no available research has addressed this question directly. A survey of states conducted in 1999 found

thirty-eight states (plus the District of Columbia) that actively reviewed rates (including but not limited to states that had statutory authority to approve rates). However, only thirteen of these states constrained rates in statute, and typically constrained rate variance for specified rate factors (such as health status), not insurer loss ratios (Kirk and Chollet 2002).

7 The price elasticity of demand is defined as the percentage change in the quantity demanded per 1 percent change in the price. The income elasticity of demand is defined as the percentage change in the quantity demanded per 1 percent change in income.

8 To estimate the price elasticity of demand among workers, Marquis and Long (1995) identified workers in the March and May 1988 CPS who did not have access to employer coverage. They imputed health status to these workers from the Survey of Income and Program Participation (SIPP) and assigned health insurance prices to worker observations based on one major commercial insurer's standard rates, varied by zip code. These imputation methods entail potentially serious problems, possibly the most serious being the imputation of standard health insurance rates without adjusting for the likelihood of higher quoted rates or denial, or even controlling for imputed self-reported health status. Moreover, the analysis supposes a standard product design that may not have been available to some consumers.

9 Young and Wildsmith (2002) reported individual premiums that average (nationally) more than $3,200 per person for individuals over age 55, and more than $5,500 for families over age 55. Gabel *et al.* (2002) estimated that at 200 percent of federal poverty, the top 25 percent of health care users with individual coverage would spend 11 percent of the income out of pocket for medical services, in addition to the premium amount.

Pauly and Nichols (2002) observed a steep income gradient in purchase of individual coverage, based on 2000–2001 data from the Community Tracking Survey. Among adults over age 24, those with income greater than 400 percent of poverty were 70–75 percent more likely to have individual insurance than those with income between 200 percent and 400 percent of poverty.

10 Using the 1997 National Survey of America's Families (NSAF) and controlling for the characteristics of the enrolled population, Brennan (2000) concluded that the employer-insured and the individually insured populations are similar in most measures of either access or utilization. However, he did find some significant differences that appeared not to translate to greater utilization on the whole. For example, individually insured persons were less likely to have a usual source of care (perhaps reflecting lower enrollment in managed care), less confident about their ability to access care, and less likely to have visited a doctor. Conversely, individually insured women more likely to have had standard preventive care in the past year than the employer-insured population.

11 Early research on small-group underwriting (Glazner *et al.* 1994) suggested that insurer underwriting (specifically, denial of coverage) may have little impact on the ultimate risk composition of insured lives in large risk pools – although it may be of considerable value to the majority of insurers that each (and collectively) writes a very small volume of business.

12 Based on the proportion of people reporting both individual and group health insurance in the same year, Chollet (2000) estimated that the lapse rate for individual coverage may be as much as ten times as high in the individual market as in the group market. However, this estimate does not account for individuals who may move between group policies during the year owing to changes in employment or plan options, nor does it account for possible movement among individual policies.

13 Hall (2001) reports that some states constrain insurers from separately rating different blocks of business in the individual market or limit how insurers may define blocks, how many blocks they may carry, or how widely they may vary rates among blocks.

14 However, available evidence in Florida indicates insurers in that state have not done so – at least not so successfully as to systematically drive relative prices. An unpublished 1999 Lewin Group report to the Florida Division of Health Care concluded that the risk composition in insurers' basic and standard product in Florida was not significantly different from the risk composition of the insured population overall.

15 People who are able to obtain coverage only by claiming federal or state protections – HIPAA or other state guaranteed conversion from group to individual coverage – are in less preferred risk categories and may pay very high prices for coverage. Premiums charged to federally eligible individuals have been reported as high as 600 percent to 2,000 percent of standard rates (Pollitz *et al.* 2000). Hall (2001) also reported that insurers had "intensified" their rating and underwriting practices in response to HIPAA.

16 To date, twenty-two states have complied with this provision of HIPAA by guaranteeing access to a state high-risk pool. Other states guaranteed issue of all individual market products (the federal fallback) to HIPAA eligibles. Still others guaranteed access to a designated statewide insurer of last resort, to conversion products, or to some other private coverage.

17 Federal laws passed after HIPAA included a number of other requirements related to maternity coverage, and coverage for cancer and mental health. As of December 1999, HCFA had notified twenty states and the District of Columbia about concerns that their statutes may not conform to federal law regarding these provisions (US GAO 2000).

18 As of 1999, sixteen states required all insurers in the individual market to guarantee issue of either all products (seven states) or of a "basic and standard" product (nine states). These provisions apply to all persons. In contrast, some other states (for example, Iowa and Oregon) guaranteed issue of some or all products only to people who are previously and continuously insured, as per HIPAA's requirement.

In 1999, thirty-four states restricted look-backs for pre-existing condition exclusions, usually to six or twelve months; and thirty-five states limited waiting periods for coverage of preexisting conditions, typically to twelve months. Only thirteen states prohibited insurers in the individual market from issuing exclusion riders that permanently exclude coverage for specific conditions for the life of the contract. While, in some states, interpretation of state law banning discrimination in the conduct of insurance may effectively curtail insurers from issuing riders to exclude coverage of maternity services or services for other specific conditions, this interpretation of state law appears to be rare (Kirk and Chollet 2002).

19 New Mexico enacted new access to its small-employer health insurance purchasing cooperative where plans are community rated for federally eligible individuals. Georgia, Florida, and Ohio strengthened their conversion laws to guarantee people leaving group plans access to better coverage for more affordable premiums than they could get prior to HIPAA.

20 Relatively few states limit insurers' rating practices in the individual market. In 1999, sixteen states limited insurers' rating for health status; of these, eight states prohibited all rating for health status (that is, they required "community rating"). Nine states prohibited insurers from rating for individuals' age, and seven more states restricted the extent to which insurers can vary rates for age (variously, from 1.5 : 1 to 5 : 1).

21 For example, the District of Columbia, Maryland, North Carolina, Rhode Island, Virginia, and West Virginia.

22 For example, Louisiana, Nevada, North Dakota, New Mexico, Oklahoma, Utah, and Washington.

23 The impact on the rate of private insurance coverage was consistent, but insignificant.

24 Chollet, Kirk, and Simon (2000) found no significant impacts on market structure from state laws requiring guaranteed issue, limiting waiting periods for coverage of pre-existing condition exclusions, prohibiting or limiting insurers' from rating for health status, or from the presence of a high-risk pool in the state.

25 This study also included measures of insurance supply. While no measure of supply affected coverage significantly, all estimated coefficients were consistent with both greater market concentration and (indepencently) the entry of HMOs yielding lower prices and greater coverage.

26 Looking at changes in the individual market nationwide, Chollet (2003) concluded that adults insured in the individual market were significantly older in 2001 than in 1995, probably owing to a more robust economy providing a growing number of young workers employment-based coverage.

References

Brennan, N. (2000) "Health Insurance Coverage of the Near Elderly." *New Federalism: National Survey of America's Families*, Series B, No. B-21, Washington, DC: Urban Institute.

Chollet, D.J. (2000) "Consumers, Insurers, and Market Behavior." *Journal of Health Politics, Policy and Law*, 25 (1): 27–44.

Chollet, D.J. (2001) "Assessing the Individual Health Insurance Market in the Post-HIPAA Era: A Review of the Literature." Report to the Assistant Secretary for Planning and Evaluation, Washington, DC: US Department of Health and Human Services.

Chollet, D.J. (2003) "Changes in the Individual Health Insurance Market." Presented at the annual meeting of AcademyHealth, Washington, DC, June 23.

Chollet, D.J. and Kirk, A.M. (1998) "Understanding Individual Health Insurance Markets: Structure, Practices and Products in Ten States." Report to the Kaiser Family Foundation, Menlo Park, CA.

Chollet, D.J. and Mays, G.M. (2002) "Leaving the Game: Insurer Withdrawals from Group and Individual Health Insurance Markets." Presentation to the Academy for Health Services Research and Health Policy, Annual Research Meeting, Washington, DC.

Chollet, D.J. and Paul, R.R. (1994) "Community Rating: Issues and Experience." Report to the Robert Wood Johnson Foundation's State Initiatives in Health Care Reform Program, Washington, DC: Alpha Center.

Chollet, D.J. and Schone E. (2002) "Expanding Health Insurance Coverage: High Risk Pools and Market Regulation." Working paper, Mathematica Policy Research, Washington, DC.

Chollet, Deborah J., Kirk, Adele M., and Chow, Marc E. (2000) "Mapping State Health Insurance Markets: Structure and Change in the States' Group and Individual Health Insurance Markets, 1995–1997." Washington, DC: Academy for Health Services Research and Health Policy, State Coverage Initiative, available at http://www.statecoverage.net/pdf/mapping.pdf (accessed March 9, 2004).

Chollet, D.J., Kirk, A.M., and Simon, K.I. (2000) "The Impact of Access Regulation on Health Insurance Market Structure." Report to the Office of the Assistant Secretary for Planning and Evaluation, Washington, DC: US Department of Health and Human Services.

Chollet, D.J., Simon, K.I., and Kirk, A.M. (2000) "What Impact HIPAA? State Regulation and Private Health Insurance Coverage Among Adults." Report to the Office of the Assistant Secretary for Planning and Evaluation, Washington, DC: US Department of Health and Human Services.

Chollet, D., Smieliauskas, F., and. Konig, M. (2003) "Mapping State Health Insurance Markets 2001: Structure and Change." Robert Wood Johnson Foundation's State Coverage Initiatives Program, Washington, DC: AcademyHealth.

Fronstin, P. (2003) "Sources of Health Insurance and Characteristics of the Uninsured: Analysis of the March 2002 Current Population Survey." Washington, DC: Employee Benefit Research Institute.

Gabel, J., Dhont, K., Whitmore, H., and Pickreign, J. (2002) "Individual Insurance: How much Financial Protection does it Provide?" in J.K. Iglehart (ed.), *Health Affairs* (Web Exclusives), Millwood, VA: Project HOPE.

Glazner, J., Braithwaite, W.R., Hull, S., and Lezotte, D.C. (1994) "The Questionable Value of Medical Screening in the Small Group Health Insurance Market." Working paper, University of Colorado Health Sciences Center.

Haley, J. and Zuckerman, S. (2000) "Health Insurance, Access, and Use: United States." Washington, DC: Urban Institute (http://www.urban.org/Uploadedpdf/discussion00-14.pdf).

Hall, M.A. (2000a) "An Evaluation of New York's Reform Law." *Journal of Health Politics, Policy and Law*, 25 (1): 71–100.

Hall, M.A. (2000b) "An Evaluation of Vermont's Reform Law." *Journal of Health Politics, Policy and Law*, 25 (1): 101–132.

Hall, M.A. (2001) "The Structure and Enforcement of Health Insurance Rating Reforms." *Inquiry*, 37 (4): 376–388.

Kirk, A.M. (2000) "Riding the Bull: Reform in Washington, Kentucky and Massachusetts." *Journal of Health Politics, Policy and Law*, 25 (1): 133–174.

Kirk, A.M. and Chollet, D.J. (2002) "State Review of Major Medical Health Insurance Rates." *Journal of Insurance Regulation*, 20: 3–18.

Marquis, M.S. and Long, S.H. (1995) "Worker Demand for Health Insurance in the Non-group Market." *Journal of Health Economics*, 14 (1): 47–63.

Monheit, A.C., Cantor, J.C., Koller, M., and Fox, K.S. (2004) "Community Rating and Sustainable Individual Health Insurance Markets" in New Jersey *Health Affairs*, 23(4). In press.

Pauly, M.V. and Herring, B.J. (1999) *Pooling Health Insurance Risks*. Washington, DC: AEI Press.

Pauly, M.V. and Nichols, L.M. (2002) "The Nongroup Health Insurance Market: Short on Facts, Long on Opinions and Policy Disputes" in J.K. Iglehart (ed.), *Health Affairs* (Web Exclusives), Millwood, VA: Project HOPE.

Pauly, M.V. and Percy, A.M. (2000) "Cost and Performance: A Comparison of the Individual and Group Health Insurance Markets." *Journal of Health Politics, Policy and Law*, 25 (1): 9–26.

Pollitz, K. (2003) Personal communication.

Pollitz, Karen and Sorian, Richard (2002) "Ensuring Health Security: Is the

Individual Market ready for Prime Time?" *Health Affairs* (Web Exclusives), 23 October: W372–W376.

Pollitz, K., Sorian, R., and Thomas, K. (2001) "How Accessible is Individual Health Insurance for Consumers in Less-than-perfect Health?" www.kff.org/content/2001/20010620a/report.pdf (accessed April 5, 2003).

Pollitz, K., Tapay, N., Hadley, E., and Specht, J. (2000) "Early Experience with 'New Federalism' in Health Insurance Regulation." *Health Affairs*, 19 (4): 7–22.

Stroupe, K.T., Kinney, E.D., and Kniesner, T.J.J. (2000) "Does Chronic Illness Affect the Adequacy of Health Insurance Coverage?" *Journal of Health Politics, Policy and Law*, 25 (2): 309–339.

Swartz, K. and Garnick, D.W. (1999) "Can Adverse Selection be Avoided in a Market for Individual Health Insurance?" *Medical Care Research and Review*, 56 (3): 373–388.

Swartz, K. and Garnick, D.W. (2000) "Lessons from New Jersey." *Journal of Health Politics, Policy and Law*, 25 (1): 45–70.

US General Accounting Office (1997) *Private Health Insurance: Millions Relying on Individual Market Face Cost and Coverage Trade-offs*. GAO/HEHS-97-8.

Vistnes, J.P. and Monheit, A.C. (1997) "Health Insurance Status of the US Civilian Noninstitutionalized Population." *MEPS Research Findings No. 1*. AHCPR Pub. No. 97-0030. Rockville, MD: Agency for Health Care Policy and Research.

Young, D.A. and Wildsmith, T.F. (2002) "Expanding Coverage: Maintain a Role for the Individual Market" In J.K. Iglehart (ed.), *Health Affairs* (Web Exclusives), Millwood, VA: Project HOPE.

Zuckerman, S. and Rajan, S. (1999) "An Alternative Approach to Measuring the Effects of Insurance Market Reforms." *Inquiry*, 36 (1): 44–56.

Part II

Responses to findings on insurance market reform

4 What can we learn from the research on small-group health insurance reform?

Thomas C. Buchmueller

In the early 1990s, nearly every state in the United States enacted new regulations governing the sale of insurance to small-employer groups. Twenty-five states also passed similar laws aimed at reforming the market for individual (i.e., non-group) health insurance. Both types of reforms were intended to increase insurance coverage by proscribing insurer underwriting and marketing practices that discriminated against high-risk groups and individuals.

The strength of the reforms varied considerably, ranging from laws that essentially codified standard practice and imposed few new constraints on insurers to laws that dramatically altered the rules of the game. New York and New Jersey stand out as the two states with the strongest reform legislation. New York's law, enacted in 1993, prohibits insurers from denying coverage to any small group or individual and requires that premiums be community-rated. That is, for a given policy, all subscribers must be charged the same price, regardless of age, sex, or any other predictor of expected medical expenditures. New Jersey's law also requires health insurance to be sold on a guaranteed issue, community-rated basis in the individual market. In the small-group market, New Jersey's law allows premiums to vary according to age, gender, and business location.

Not surprisingly, strong reforms like New York's and New Jersey's generated considerable controversy. Insurance industry groups and other critics of government regulation argued that community rating laws actually reduced insurance coverage via an "adverse selection death spiral." According to this argument, insurance regulations that benefit high-risk (i.e., older, sicker) consumers raise premiums for low-risk (younger, healthier) ones. If low-risk consumers respond to these higher prices by dropping coverage, insurers must raise premiums to account for the deterioration of the risk pool. This, in turn, leads to an unraveling of the market.

One insurance industry-sponsored group, the Council for Affordable Health Insurance, commissioned the consulting firm of Milliman & Robertson to study the impact of New York's community rating law. The report by Milliman & Robertson showed that insurance coverage declined in the state after the law went into effect, which they interpreted as empirical support for the death spiral hypothesis (Litow and Davidoff 1994). In a report published by the Health Insurance Association of America (HIAA), Custer (1998) uses cross-sectional data from 1998 to compare insurance coverage rates in states that did and did not enact guaranteed issue and rating reforms. The data show lower rates of coverage in states with those regulations which Custer interpreted as supporting industry arguments that the regulations reduced insurance coverage.

The Milliman & Robertson report received considerable attention in the media and may have influenced policy developments in other states (Lieberman 1995). The president of the HIAA cited the Custer report in testimony before Congress (Kahn 1999). However, policymakers would be well advised to ignore both studies, as they are seriously flawed. The Milliman & Robertson analysis makes no attempt to distinguish any effect of New York's community rating law from the longer-term decline in insurance in the state and the rest of the United States. This is critical, given that private insurance coverage had been falling nationwide for several years prior to 1993. The fact that the number of people covered in New York's small-group and individual markets fell by 2.4 percent in the twelve months immediately after the community rating law went into effect would appear to support the death spiral hypothesis. However, when we consider that the same data source shows that coverage fell by nearly 9 percent in the six months preceding the reform, this interpretation seems less compelling. Furthermore, coverage fell not only for commercial insurers, which had made extensive use of the underwriting strategies that were outlawed by New York's law, but also for the state's Blue Cross and Blue Shield plans, which had always charged community-rated premiums. Since the new regulations did not change the way the Blues did business, it is unlikely that they caused them to lose business. The HIAA/Custer report has a slightly different but equally serious flaw. The cross-sectional comparison that is at the heart of that analysis ignores the fact that insurance coverage was lower in states that enacted strong reforms long before the legislation was enacted.

In the past several years, a number of academic studies have also examined the impact of the state-level small-group reforms. These studies recognize the difficulty of identifying causal effects of reform legislation. Most do a careful job of attempting to distinguish reform effects from secular trends driven by other factors influencing health care and labor markets and from pre-existing differences between states choosing different policy paths. As a result, these studies have the potential to inform public policy. However, the empirical challenges are nontrivial, and the different studies achieve varying degrees of success in overcoming them to identify causal effects of the small-group reforms.

In order to determine what policymakers can learn from these studies it is necessary to first understand several critical methodological issues. This chapter discusses these methodological issues with an eye toward evaluating the scholarly research on the impacts of small-group reform. The goal is to identify the key assumptions that determine the validity of individual studies and to provide a framework for evaluating divergent results across studies. Since most studies test for the effect of state-level small-group reforms on insurance coverage, the methodological issues discussed in the next three sections will be framed in terms of this outcome. I will argue that the best evidence from the literature suggests that these reforms had essentially no effect on the number of Americans with insurance coverage. In the fifth section I review several possible explanations for this result. Concluding remarks are in the final section.

What is the counterfactual?

To convincingly estimate the effect of a public policy like small-group health insurance regulations, it is necessary to predict what would have happened if the policy had not been enacted. As noted, the fact that the small-group reforms of the 1990s were enacted against the backdrop of declining insurance coverage rates makes this a challenging empirical problem. States that didn't pass reform legislation represent a possible "control group" whose experiences can be treated as a counterfactual against which outcomes in reform states can be compared. As in a clinical trial, the validity of this contrast depends on the similarity of the treatment group and the control group. Comparisons of neighboring states that have similar demographics and are subject to shared macroeconomic shocks make for the most credible contrasts. In contrast, a comparison of two states in different regions and having very different populations provides less convincing evidence.

Since only five states (Alabama, Hawaii, Michigan, Pennsylvania, and the District of Columbia) did not enact any reforms, the set of potential controls is limited. Studies that use national data essentially compare trends in states that enacted reforms with these five states as a group. Unfortunately, these studies generally do not provide any evidence of how these two groups of states compare to each other in terms of insurance coverage rates in the pre-reform period, population demographics, economic conditions, or other factors likely to influence coverage trends. Thus, it is not clear how well these non-reform states as a group approximate what would have happened in all other states if there had been no reforms.

Even when good controls exist, estimated policy effects may be sensitive to the period over which changes in outcomes are measured. Figure 4.1 presents data on private insurance coverage in New York and Pennsylvania for the period from 1987 to 1996.[1] As noted, New York enacted very strong reforms in 1993, while Pennsylvania was one of the few states with no reforms. If we aggregate the data into two periods, one consisting of the years prior to 1993 and the other consisting of the years after, we see

Figure 4.1 Trends in private health insurance coverage in New York and Pennsylvania, 1987–1996.

that coverage fell by 2.6 percentage points in New York, compared to only 1.6 percentage points in Pennsylvania.[2] This one percentage point difference, which is statistically significant, would appear to suggest that New York's community rating law did, in fact, reduce insurance coverage.

However, a visual inspection of the data in Figure 4.1 cautions against this interpretation. Whereas in 1990 the two states had nearly identical coverage rates, in the following year coverage fell by two percentage points in New York and increased by one percentage point in Pennsylvania, resulting in a three percentage point gap between the two states. It is not clear what explains this divergence, but since it occurred two years prior to New York's reform, it obviously cannot be attributed to that legislation. From 1991 on, the two graphs are roughly parallel. Thus if we define the pre-reform period as the years 1991 to 1993, we see no statistically significant difference in the trends for the two states.[3]

The sensitivity of estimated policy effects to the definition of the pre- and post-intervention periods is an issue that is largely unexamined in the small-group reform literature. Generally, studies neither justify their choice of years to analyze nor consider whether their results change when alternative time windows are used. While studies differ in the time periods analyzed, it is not possible to determine the extent to which this affects the results because of larger differences across studies in research design.

Accounting for the targeted nature of the reforms

Because the data in Figure 4.1 pertain to all non-elderly people in New York and Pennsylvania, they ignore an important feature of the reforms enacted in New York and elsewhere, which is that they apply only to employer-sponsored groups of fifty or fewer employees. The fact that after 1990 there is no discernible difference in the trends for the two states may mean that New York's reforms had no impact on insurance coverage. Alternatively, this result may be an artifact of a poorly defined treatment group. Perhaps there was a large effect on the number of people obtaining coverage through small groups or as individuals, but this effect is obscured by pooling such individuals with employees of large firms, who should not have been directly affected.

While some studies pool employees of small and large firms in this way (Sloan and Conover 1998; Zuckerman and Rajan 1999), others recognize that since larger firms should not have been impacted by the regulations, they represent an alternative control group for teasing out causal effects (Buchmueller and DiNardo 2002; Simon 2002; Monheit and Schone 2004). Multiple control groups allow several possible estimates of a treatment effect and thereby provide a means of testing the robustness and "face validity" of research results. In general, there is no single "right" estimate, though in some circumstances one contrast may be preferred to another. For example, if we believe that state-specific shocks are very important, large firms from states that enacted reforms may represent a better control group than small firms in non-reform states. On the other hand, one might argue that because of important differences between large and small firms, the workers they employ and the markets in which they purchase insurance, small firms in non-reform states represent the best control group for assessing the effects of small-group reform.

The cleanest "natural experiments" are ones where alternative contrasts yield similar results and where treatment effects are driven mainly by changes for the treatment group. In contrast, it is difficult to draw clear conclusions when estimates based on different control groups diverge or when results are driven by unexplained changes in groups that did not receive the treatment. Table 4.1, reproduced from Simon (2002), illustrates such a difficult inference problem. The table presents insurance coverage rates for employees of small and large firms in "full reform" and four "non-reform" states before and after reforms were in place.[4] From these cross-tabs we can calculate several alternative estimates of the reform effect. Coverage fell by similar amounts (between 2 and 2.5 percentage points) for three of the four groups. Thus, a comparison of the trend for employees of small firms in full-reform states to employees in large firms in the same states suggests that the reforms had no effect on coverage. In contrast, using small firms in non-reform states as the control group implies that the reforms reduced coverage.[5]

Table 4.1 Trends in private insurance coverage in reform and non-reform states, 1991 and 1996 (%)

Type of state	*Period*		*Difference*
	Pre-reform (1991)	*Post-reform (1996)*	
1 Full-reform			
(a) Small firms	39.4	37.4	−2.0
(b) Large firms	75.8	73.7	−2.1
2 Non-reform			
(a) Small firms	47.2	47.0	−0.1
(b) Large firms	79.6	77.4	−2.3
Differences			
Full-reform, small–large (1a–1b)	−32.4	−30.3	0.1
Small firms, reform–non-reform (1a–2a)	−7.8	−9.7	−1.8

Source: Simon (2002).

To conclude from these data that small-group reform legislation led to a reduction in insurance coverage is to say that if the reforms had not been enacted coverage would have stabilized for small firms in reform states while continuing to fall among large firms in the same states as well as for large firms in non-reform states. While possible, this story is not especially compelling. The main reason is that the negative reform effect is driven by the unique trend (or lack thereof) for small firms in the four non-reform states.

Accounting for differential treatment effects

There is another potentially important contrast within reform states. To the extent that new small-group insurance regulations had any bite, they should have had quite different effects on high-risk consumers – whom they were designed to benefit by lowering the cost of insurance – and low-risk consumers – who may have ended up facing higher premiums as a result of these laws. In addition to being of direct policy interest, testing for such differential effects provides an additional way to distinguish true causal effects from spurious correlation. That is, if small-group reforms did reduce coverage, the declines should be greatest for low-risk consumers. However, while this prediction is straightforward, limitations of the available data make it difficult to test.

A convincing test requires a measure of risk that insurers used in underwriting prior to reform but were prohibited from using afterwards. Unfortunately, the types of health conditions that may result in higher premiums or outright exclusions in unregulated markets are not observed in the data sets that are available and meet other necessary requirements for this type of analysis. The March CPS is the data source that has been most commonly used to analyze health insurance coverage in general and is the data set used in several studies on small-group reform (Sloan and Conover 1998; Marsteller *et al.* 1998; Zuckerman and Rajan 1999; Buchmueller and DiNardo 2002; Simon 2002). For the relevant time period, the best risk proxies available in the CPS are age and gender. While these variables are correlated with expected medical care use, they are not useful for defining risk categories that are relevant to small-group health insurance reforms because, in nearly every state that enacted reforms, insurers can still use them in setting premiums. Thus, for most states, there is no reason to expect reforms to cause premiums to rise more for a 25-year-old than for a 60-year-old.

The one exception to this argument is New York with its community rating law. New York's 1993 reform legislation had a large and immediate impact on premiums in the individual and small-group markets. According to data from the state Department of Insurance, 40 percent of individuals saw their premiums rise by 20 percent or more, while 18 percent saw their premiums fall by a comparable amount. As would be expected, prices increased the most for younger consumers and decreased the most for older ones. According to newspaper reports, one indemnity insurer, Mutual of Omaha, raised rates for men under the age of 30 by 170 percent. Price changes appear to have been less dramatic in the small-group market because of the pooling of older and younger workers within firms. Nonetheless, the data show that New York's law eliminated pre-existing premium differences between groups of relatively younger and older workers.

This situation provides a clean test for the hypothesis that community rating reduces coverage by driving lower-risk consumers from the market. The death spiral hypothesis predicts that younger consumers should be more likely than older ones to drop insurance coverage, causing the age distribution of the insured population to shift to the right (i.e., get older). In fact, John DiNardo and I show that such a shift did occur among individuals insured in New York's small-group and individual health insurance markets. However, we also show that essentially identical changes occurred in Pennsylvania and for employees of large firms in New York. Rather than implying a negative effect of New York's health insurance reforms, this pattern suggests that whatever factors that caused coverage to fall nationwide had a disproportionate effect on younger consumers.[6] Likewise, separate regressions by age group provide no indication that New York's community rating law caused younger adults to drop insurance coverage.

In her study using national data, Simon (2002) chooses a slightly different risk proxy and obtains very different results. She defines single men under age 35 as the low-risk group and married women with children as high risk. Her regression results for the single men indicate that full reform is associated with a decline of 6.4 percentage points, which is a huge effect given the relatively low level of baseline coverage for young men working in small firms. In contrast, she finds a statistically insignificant increase in insurance coverage for the married women. She interprets this difference as evidence that the small-group reforms reduced coverage by inducing adverse selection.[7]

The problem with this interpretation is that, as just mentioned, most reforms did not outlaw the use of age or gender in underwriting. The distinction between single individuals and married adults with children is even more meaningless, as even in New York insurers are still allowed to charge more for families than for single coverage. Thus comparisons between these risk categories do not provide a meaningful test. Moreover, the fact that the comparison of New York and Pennsylvania provides no evidence of a differential effect across age groups (a result that Simon confirms in her data), means that her finding of a negative effect using national data is being driven by either (1) changes in other states with weaker reforms that allow insurers much greater flexibility in setting premiums, or (2) unexplained trends in the other non-reform states. There is no plausible theoretical explanation for why laws that did little to change insurer behavior should have a larger impact than a law that brought about major changes and, as mentioned before, we should be suspicious of estimated treatment effects that are driven by idiosyncratic trends for a control group.

Monheit and Schone (2004) take a similar, though more nuanced, approach to testing for differential effects by consumer risk status. Since the data sets they use include information on health status and medical care utilization, they are able to create a risk proxy based on expected medical expenditures. This is a more relevant concept of risk than age and sex, though their measure is strongly influenced by those variables as well. One of the nice things about this paper is that they present a number of different regression specifications, which shows how the results vary depending on how treatment and control groups are defined. The majority of their results indicate no statistically significant effect of small-group reform for either low-risk or high-risk groups. In some cases the (statistically insignificant) differences between the two suggest that coverage among low risks fell relative to high risks, which is consistent with the death spiral hypothesis. However, in many cases the difference goes in the other direction, a result which is probably best explained by chance.[8]

Why did the reforms have no effect?

My reading of the literature is that the reforms enacted by states in the 1990s had essentially no effect on the number of people insured through the small-group market. This conclusion may be surprising given the attention paid to discriminatory insurer practices that motivated the reforms in the first place, the high expectations of some reform advocates, and the controversy that the reforms generated in some states. There are three possible (overlapping) explanations for this "non-result."

The first explanation is that the underwriting practices that motivated the reforms were never a major reason for low rates of insurance provision by small firms. Survey data suggest that prior to the reforms very few small firms did not offer insurance because they were denied coverage on the basis of their industry or the health status of their employees (Morrisey *et al.* 1994; Cantor *et al.* 1995). This means that the potential of the reforms to increase coverage by eliminating barriers faced by "high-risk" groups was quite limited. It also means that the potential for unintended consequences was limited as well. If very few high-risk groups were brought into small-group risk pools, the impact on premiums for low-risk groups should have been small.

It is important to note that this explanation does not rule out the possibility that some reforms delivered a significant benefit to a small number of truly high-risk consumers. Two small-scale experimental studies on regulations in the individual insurance market provide some evidence to this effect (Richardson and Hall 2001; Pollitz *et al.* 2001). In both studies, researchers approached insurance brokers and agents posing as consumers with health problems of varying severity. While small samples prevent precise statistical tests, the results indicate that in less regulated markets consumers with moderate health problems face some difficulty obtaining insurance while people with very serious conditions face severe access problems, whereas the same people were able to obtain coverage in markets with strong regulations. Because of the small number of people affected and the limited information on health status in the national data sets used to analyze the state level reforms, it is impossible to quantify the magnitude of such effects.

A second explanation for the fact that the small-group reforms did not appear to affect coverage is that in many states the laws had little "bite" – i.e., they did not substantially alter insurer practices. Rating rules are one area where insurers have retained considerable flexibility. Nearly every state reform allows premiums to vary with demographic characteristics, such as age and sex, and many allow further variation within demographic cells. For example, Ohio's law requires premiums to be no more than 35 percent above or below a plan's standard rate (Hall 2000/2001). This can translate to a more than 100 percent difference between the premium charged the highest- and lowest-risk groups within a demographic category (1.35/0.65), which encompasses most of the spread that would occur in an unregulated market.[9]

There are other ways that insurers in reform states are able to avoid the intent of the new regulations. For example, in a number of states, insurers are required to sell only one or two products on a guaranteed issue basis.

If these plans can be underwritten separately from other products, as is often the case, the premiums will adjust to reflect the cost of high-risk groups that insurers prefer not to insure (Hall 2000/2001). Even if it is possible to regulate the benefit design and pricing of such products, there is no practical way to require insurers to market them with any vigor.

Of course, not all state level reforms were weak or riddled with loopholes. In particular, New York's imposition of pure community rating represents a radical change in rate-setting policy relative to an unreformed market. As noted, there is considerable evidence that the imposition of community rating in New York dramatically altered the distribution of premiums, raising rates significantly for younger, healthier consumers. According to media reports, some carriers that previously had a large share of the small-group and individual markets experienced large declines in enrollment. Why then, don't the CPS data show a reduction in health insurance coverage among young adults?

The third possible explanation, which applies to states like New York, is that when new regulations caused premiums to rise for lower-risk groups they looked for alternative, less costly forms of insurance rather than dropping coverage altogether. If there were certain plans that were relatively unattractive to higher-risk consumers, say because they offered less generous coverage or were perceived to impose greater restrictions on patients, lower-risk consumers could have avoided large premium increases by switching to those plans.

In fact, there is good evidence that this type of sorting led to an increase in HMO penetration in New York's small-group and individual markets in the wake of that state's reforms. Data from several employer surveys indicate that, after 1993, the percentage of small New York firms offering HMO coverage more than doubled from its pre-reform level, increasing by twenty-five percentage points. The fact that the rate of HMO penetration was constant for small firms in Pennsylvania suggests that this change is not explained by a broader trend affecting the small-group market. Similarly, the fact that there was little change in the percentage of large firms in New York offering HMO coverage to their employees (and among large firms the trends in New York and Pennsylvania are essentially identical) suggests that the change in New York's small-group market was not due to state-specific factors. While it is not possible with the data from these employer surveys to confirm that this trend in New York came about from lower-risk groups switching from indemnity to HMO coverage, other data strongly suggest that this, in fact, was the case.[10] Other research using data from more states also suggests a relationship between small-group reforms and HMO penetration (Marquis and Long 2001/2002; Buchmueller and Liu 2003).

The notion that rules on guaranteed issue and rating restrictions would lead to a shift in the type of insurance purchased is consistent with the most relevant economic theory concerning regulation and competition in insurance markets (Rothschild and Stiglitz 1976) and with results from a number of settings where health insurance choices are made at the individual level and prices do not vary with risk (Buchmueller 1998; Cutler and Reber 1998; Yegian *et al.* 2000; Strombom *et al.* 2002). In these examples, as in New York, adverse selection within a market caused certain insurance plans to lose considerable enrollment as lower-risk consumers left the plan in response to rising premiums. However, since those consumers migrated to other plans, there was no adverse selection against the market. This distinction is important, though it often receives insufficient attention.

Adverse selection within a market can lead to a new "separating" equilibrium, in which high and low risks sort to different plans. Or it can lead to a situation where risk pools are continuously broken up as low risks defect for lower-cost options and plans that are left with high risks fail. This type of unstable market dynamic was one of the motivations for the state-level small-group reforms in the first place. Unfortunately, it is not possible with the data sources that are available to say whether small-group health insurance markets are more or less stable than before the reforms.

What can we learn from the research on small-group health insurance reform?

The state-level small-group reforms of the 1990s reflect the incremental approach taken by both the states and the federal government with regard to health insurance. The goal of these policies was to reduce the number of Americans without health insurance and improve the stability and affordability of insurance for those with coverage. Their limited scope reflects the lack of consensus on the issue of universal insurance coverage, which translated to a lack of broad political support for large-scale initiatives, especially those involving explicit redistribution. In this context, small-group reforms were politically feasible because they involved no direct outlay of public funds and they targeted insurer business practices that were viewed as unfair and socially undesirable (even if they could be justified on economic grounds).

The fact that the reforms had essentially no effect on the number of Americans with health insurance says as much about the nature of the uninsured problem in the United States and the potential for incremental policies to address the problem as it does about the specific features of the various state laws or the role of regulation in insurance markets. While there is some debate among policy analysts about whether health insurance is "affordable" for the uninsured (See Levy and DeLeire 2002 and Bundorf and Pauly 2003, for example), there is reasonable consensus that demand-side rather than supply-side factors are the primary reason that so many people lack coverage. According to this view, universal or near-universal coverage can be achieved only with a combination of public subsidies and some kind of requirement that people obtain health insurance. It is not reasonable to expect supply-side policies, like the state-level small-group reforms, to have had a major effect on coverage.

That is not to say that there was little reason to study the reforms. Even if we could have expected their impact to be small, either a positive or a negative effect on coverage was theoretically plausible, making their actual impact an empirical question. The importance of careful, objective analysis is heightened by the high expectations of reform advocates and the strong arguments made by reform critics.

As I have described, researchers in this area face a daunting problem of disentangling the effects of the reforms from other factors that contributed to a decline in coverage over the 1980s and early 1990s. In the last part of the 1990s, trends in macroeconomic conditions and health care inflation were quite favorable for insurance coverage. More recently, as the economy has faltered and health care cost growth has accelerated, the problem of the uninsured is beginning to receive renewed attention.

In some states this has led to new legislation concerning the small-group market. One example is Colorado, which passed legislation that will undo parts of the reforms it enacted in the 1990s by allowing insurers greater flexibility in setting rates. One factor motivating the legislation was a 23 percent decline in the number of individuals covered through small-group plans in the state between 2000 and 2002.[11] A careful reading of the evidence concerning earlier reforms provides no support for the argument that this trend was the direct result of Colorado's small-group regulations. Rather, the fact that the state's unemployment rate roughly doubled over this period is a much more likely explanation. Therefore, there is little reason to expect insurance coverage to increase as a result of this new legislation.

As Colorado is rolling back its small-group insurance regulations, legislation proposed in Michigan would move in the other direction. Bills have been proposed in both the state House and Senate that would introduce premium rate bands for commercial insurers selling in the small-group market. The state's Blue Cross plan, which as the insurer of last resort is required to community-rate, would be allowed to set rates in the same manner. Not surprisingly, these proposals are supported by Blue Cross Blue Shield of Michigan and opposed by the commercial insurers with which they compete. The lesson from the research on earlier small-group reforms is that the proposed legislation would have a greater impact on how market share is divided between different insurers than on the overall rate of insurance coverage.

Notes

1 The data are from the March Current Population Survey (CPS), the most common source of information on insurance coverage and the data used in many of the studies on small-group reform. See Buchmueller and DiNardo (2002) for more details.

2 For the period 1987 to 1993, the average coverage rate was 50.5 percent in New York and 52.5 percent in Pennsylvania. For the post-reform period of 1994 to 1996 the corresponding figures are 47.9 percent and 50.9 percent, respectively.
3 In this shorter pre-reform period, the average coverage rates were 48.1 percent in New York and 50.7 percent in Pennsylvania.
4 The full reform group consists of thirty five states that require at least some policies be sold on a guaranteed issue basis and restrict the variation in premiums. Non-reform states in this analysis are Alabama, Michigan, Pennsylvania, and the District of Columbia. See Simon (2002) for more details.
5 Comparing the trend for small firms in reform states to either small firms in other states or large firms in the reform states produces alternative "difference-in-differences" (DD) estimates. Both control groups can be used to create a "difference-in-difference-in-difference" (DDD) estimate, which essentially compares the relative trend between small and large firms in reform states to the comparable difference in non-reform states. In this case, the DDD estimate is essentially the same as the DD estimate based on small firms in reform and non-reform states because the trends are virtually identical for large firms in the two categories.
6 That coverage has fallen more for younger adults than for older ones is not surprising. Recent research suggests that the decline in employer-sponsored insurance coverage from the mid-1980s to the mid-1990s is largely explained by a decrease in employee take-up in response to rising premium contributions (Cooper and Schone 1997; Cutler 2002). Other research shows that younger employees have a substantially more elastic demand for insurance than older employees (Royalty and Solomon 1999; Strombom *et al.* 2002).
7 Sloan and Conover (1998) interact age dummies with variables denoting states that limit the use of age in setting individual and small-group premiums. They find no significant effect of these rules on the coverage of either younger or older adults. It is difficult to compare their results to Simon's because of a number of other differences in their empirical specification.
8 Monheit and Schone report 108 possible "effects," of which only three are statistically significant at the 95 percent confidence level. Assuming that the true effect is zero, we would expect five or six of these effects to be statistically significant purely by random error.
9 Nichols and Pauly (2002) report data on the non-group premiums offered to potential subscribers by one insurer in a completely unregulated market. Nearly 80 percent of individuals seeking coverage from that firm received premium quotes that were no more than 25 percent higher than the lowest rate offered by the firm.
10 See Buchmueller and DiNardo (2002) for more details.
11 The source of these figures is a March 12, 2003, press release from the Colorado Department of Regulatory Agencies.

References

Buchmueller, T.C. (1998) "Does a Fixed-dollar Contribution Lower Spending?" *Health Affairs*, 17: 228–235.

Buchmueller, T.C. and DiNardo, John (2002) "Did Community Rating Induce an Adverse Selection Death Spiral? Evidence from New York, Pennsylvania and Connecticut." *American Economic Review*, 92 (1): 280–294.

Buchmueller, T.C. and Liu, Su (2003) "Health Insurance Reform and HMO Penetration in the Small Group Market." Unpublished manuscript, University of California, Irvine.

Bundorf, K. and Pauly, M.V. (2003) "Is Health Insurance Affordable for the Uninsured?" Working paper 9281, Washington, DC: NBER.

Cantor, J.C., Long, S.H., and Marquis, M.S. (1995) "Private Employment-based Health Insurance in Ten States." *Health Affairs*, 14 (2): 199–211.

Cooper, P.F. and Schone, B.S. (1997) "More Offers, Fewer Takers for Employment-based Health Insurance, 1987 and 1996." *Health Affairs*, 16 (6): 142–149.

Custer, W.S. (1998) *Health Insurance Coverage and the Uninsured*, Washington, DC: Health Insurance Association of America.

Cutler, D. (forthcoming) "Employee Costs and the Decline in Health Insurance Coverage" in David M. Cutler and Alan M. Garber (eds), *Frontiers in Health Policy Research*, VI, Cambridge, MA: MIT Press.

Cutler, D. and Reber, S. (1998) "Paying for Health Insurance: The Tradeoff between Competition and Adverse Selection." *Quarterly Journal of Economics*, 113 (2): 433–466.

Hall, M.A. (2000/2001) "The Structure and Enforcement of Health Insurance Rating Reforms," *Inquiry*, 37: 376–388.

Kahn, C. (1999) "The Relationship between Health Care Costs and America's Uninsured." Testimony before the Employer/Employee Relations Subcommittee of the House Committee on Education and Workforce.

Levy, H. and DeLeire, T. (2002) "What Do People Buy when They Don't Buy Health Insurance?" Working paper, Joint Center for Poverty Research.

Lieberman, T. (1995) "This is the Story of the Vested Interest that Hired the Firm that Fronted the Study that Skewed the Numbers that Spread through the Press and Finished off a Vital Piece of Health Care Reform." *Columbia Journalism Review*, January/February: 28–33.

Litow, M. and Davidoff, D. (1994) "The Impact of Guaranteed Issue and Community Rating in the State of New York." Unpublished report, Seattle, WA: Milliman & Robertson.

Marquis, M.S. and Long, S. (2001/2002) "Effects of 'Second Generation' Small Group Health Insurance Market Reforms, 1993 to 1997." *Inquiry*, 38 (4): 365–384.

Marsteller, J., Nichols, L.M., Adam Badawi, A. *et al.* (1998) "Variations in the Uninsured: State and County Level Analyses." Unpublished manuscript, Washington, DC: Urban Institute.

Monheit, A. and Schone, B.S. (2004) "How has Small Group Market Reform affected Employee Health Insurance Coverage?" *Journal of Public Economics*, 88 (1–2): 237–254.

Morrisey, M.A., Jensen, G.A., and Morlock, R.J. (1994) "Small Employers and the Health Insurance Market." *Health Affairs*, 13 (5): 149–161.

Pauly, M.V. and Nichols, L.M. (2002) "The Nongroup Health Insurance Market: Short on Facts, Long on Opinions and Policy Disputes." *Health Affairs* (Web Exclusives), 23 October: W325–W344.

Pollitz, K., Sorian, R., and Thomas, K. (2001) "How Accessible is Individual Health Insurance for Consumers in Less-than-perfect Health?" Report, Menlo Park, CA: Kaiser Family Foundation.

Richardson, C. and Hall, M.A. (2001) "Agents' Behavior under Health Insurance Market Reforms." *Journal of Insurance Regulation*, 18: 340–361.

Rothschild, M. and Stiglitz, J. (1976) "Equilibrium in Competitive Insurance Markets." *Quarterly Journal of Economics*, 90: 630–649.

Royalty, A. and Solomon, N. (1999) "Health Plan Choice: Price Elasticities in a Managed Competition Setting." *Journal of Human Resources*, 34 (1): 1–41.

Simon, K. (2002) "Adverse Selection in Health Insurance Markets? Evidence from State Small-Group Health Insurance Reforms." Unpublished manuscript, Cornell University.

Sloan, F.A. and Conover, C.J. (1998) "Effects of State Reforms on Health Insurance Coverage of Adults." *Inquiry*, 35: 280–293.

Strombom, B., Buchmueller, T.C. and Feldstein, P. (2002) "Switching Costs, Price Sensitivity and Health Plan Choice." *Journal of Health Economics*, 21 (1): 89–116.

Yegian, J.M., Buchmueller, T.C., Smith, M., and Monroe, A. (2000) "The Health Insurance Plan of California: The First Five Years." *Health Affairs*, 19: 158–165.

Zuckerman, S. and Rajan, S. (1999) "An Alternative Approach to Measuring the Effects of Insurance Market Reforms." *Inquiry*, 36: 44–56.

5 A critical assessment of research on insurance market reform

Barbara Steinberg Schone

During the early 1990s, the majority of states enacted legislation to regulate the small-group health insurance market. These measures were aimed at improving coverage among small-firm employees and their dependents by making coverage more accessible and affordable. Reforms aimed at improving access to health insurance included provisions such as guaranteed issue, guaranteed renewability, portability, and limits on pre-existing condition restrictions; premiums associated with such coverage were regulated through rules that limited premium variability across small firms. Prior to reform, it was believed that the small-group market was subject to high premiums, medical underwriting, and restrictions on the nature of coverage – features which were all designed to avoid adverse selection.

There has been growing interest among researchers in evaluating the effects of these policies. The research on small-group market reform has concentrated mainly on the question of whether reform had its intended effects on improving access to coverage and making plans more affordable for small-group employees. In this chapter, I provide a critical review of the empirical methods that have been used to identify the effects of reform. I also discuss improvements that can be made in the future that may enhance our understanding of the effect of these policies.

The nature of small-group market reforms and their expected effects

Small-group market reforms consist of access reforms designed to increase insurance availability and rating reforms, which are aimed at controlling variation in the cost of coverage in small firms. States with the most extensive access reforms typically impose guaranteed issue, which requires that if insurers offer coverage to any small firm, then coverage must be offered to all small firms that desire coverage. There is considerable variation in the nature of guaranteed issue, with some states requiring guaranteed issue of all plans (the most comprehensive form of guaranteed issue) and other states requiring guaranteed issue of only a single plan. In addition to guaranteed issue, many states have a guaranteed renewal provision, which requires that insurers continue to offer coverage to a small firm even if it has bad claims experience. Other access measures include portability, which allows small-group employees to obtain coverage at a new firm (or with a new insurer within the same firm) without facing any new exclusion period; and pre-existing condition limitations, which limit the amount of time that individuals (or certain conditions) can be excluded from coverage. On net, these access measures should increase the value of insurance to small groups by ensuring that coverage is available currently and in the future.

All states that adopted reform have some provision to control premiums by reducing their variance. In general, two different forms of pricing restrictions are employed: rating bands and community rating (both modified and pure). Rating bands are designed to allow insurers to vary premiums up to a certain maximum amount above and below a midpoint.[1] Modified community rating, on the other hand, allows insurers to vary premiums along a number of dimensions specified in the reforms (e.g., age, industry) but does not generally allow health status to be used directly in setting premiums. Finally, pure community rating requires that premiums be set without allowing for premiums to vary by factors that are correlated with health status (e.g., age would not be allowed). While it is clear *a priori* that pure community rating will compress premiums the most, the relative compression of premiums under adjusted community rating and rating bands is unclear. Rather, details of each state's rating policies can be used to classify states as either having strict or weak rating restrictions. Table 5.1, based on Monheit and Schone (2004), shows the distribution of reform components across the states as of 1996.

Table 5.1 Frequency distribution of reform measures adopted by states

	Guaranteed issue	*Guaranteed renewal*	*Portability*	*Pre-existing conditions*	*Rating restrictions*	*No. of states (%)*
1	No	No	No	No	None	3 (6.3)
2	No	No	No	Yes	Relatively weak	1 (2.1)
3	No	Yes	No	No	Relatively weak	1 (2.1)
4	No	Yes	Yes	Yes	Relatively weak	5 (10.4)
5	No	Yes	Yes	Yes	Tight	1 (2.1)
6	Yes	Yes	Yes	Yes	Relatively weak	21 (43.8)
6A	1 Plan					2 (4.2)
6B	>1 Plan	Yes	Yes	Yes	Relatively weak	19 (39.6)
7	Yes	Yes	Yes	Yes	Tight	16 (33.3)
7A	1 Plan					3 (6.3)
7B	>1 Plan	Yes	Yes	Yes	Tight	13 (27.1)

Source: Monheit and Schone (2004).

Note
Three states (Hawaii, Washington, and the District of Columbia) are excluded from the analysis.

Theoretical expectations: what are the expected effects of small-group reform?

The intended effects of small-group reform were to improve health insurance coverage and access and to control health insurance premiums. However, as with many public policies, the actual effects of reform may deviate from their intended effects. Economic theory provides some guidance regarding the expected effects of small-group reforms. As with many policy initiatives, the overall effects of reform are ambiguous and are likely to have different effects on different population subgroups.

To assess the impact of reform requires that we consider the impact of the access measures and pricing restrictions separately and consider how reforms will impact low-risk versus high-risk firms. Access measures of reform were designed to improve insurance coverage by ensuring access currently and in the future and by restricting the limits on insurance coverage. As noted, access measures may make insurance more valuable to small groups. If the value of insurance increases, then some firms that have previously foregone coverage may now desire it. One might also expect that the access reforms may increase the demand for coverage, especially among higher-risk (and more expensive) firms.

If high-risk firms are more likely to obtain coverage after reform, then premiums may be expected to rise on average across small firms. Some lower-risk firms may also respond to the increase in premiums by dropping coverage, resulting in a further rise in average premiums. Consequently, the overall impact of access measures on insurance coverage is ambiguous and will depend on the relative behavior of high- and low-risk firms. We would, however, expect coverage to improve for high-risk firms relative to low-risk firms.

In addition to premium changes that may arise from access reforms, rating reforms may have an additional effect on premiums. As noted, all rating restrictions are intended to reduce the variance of the premium distribution.[2] Therefore, high premiums (i.e., those faced by the highest-risk firms) are expected to fall while low premiums (i.e., those faced by the lowest-risk firms) may increase, leading to cross-subsidies from low-risk to high-risk firms. One possible consequence of these cross subsidies – to the extent to which they occur – is an increase in high-risk firms that enter the small-group market and a reduction in low-risk firms in the market. The net effect of these changes would be for premiums to rise on average, further exacerbating the exit of low-risk firms. Thus, the overall effect of premium compression will depend on how sensitive high- (low)-risk groups are to falling (rising) premiums. To the extent that there are changes in coverage, we would expect premiums to rise on average and for high-risk firms to gain coverage and low-risk firms to lose coverage (with an indeterminate net effect on coverage).[3]

Empirical assessments of reform

Given the theoretical ambiguities outlined above, the actual effect of small-group market reforms on insurance outcomes becomes an empirical question. As a consequence, a small but growing literature has arisen to analyze these reforms. Overall, most studies find relatively modest effects of reform on insurance coverage. While reform has not resulted in adverse selection death spirals, as feared by critics, it has also not led to substantial improvements in insurance coverage and access as was intended.

On face value, it would seem that the take-away message from the existing studies is that reform did not have much of an impact on coverage. However, before accepting this conclusion it is important to assess the quality of the research. To do so requires a systematic review of the methodologies used and careful consideration of the issues that have not yet been adequately addressed in the literature. The literature on small-group reforms conveniently falls into two distinct groups, which I will refer to as the first- and second-generation studies.

First-generation studies

First-generation studies typically analyze the effects of reform by using time series data, in many cases with controls for aggregate time trends (Buchmueller and Jensen 1997; Sloan and Conover 1998; Jensen and Morrisey 1999; Zuckerman and Rajan 1999).[4] These studies have generally found mostly small or statistically insignificant effects of reform. The main concern with the first-generation studies of reform is the possibility that the results are biased because they do not adequately isolate the effects of reform from other factors that may have affected insurance status.

An example of the type of bias that might impact estimates of reform effects arises when cross-sectional data are used. In such cases, it is difficult to control for inherent differences across reform and non-reform states. For example, if unobservable differences across states (e.g., nuances of the insurance market that affect coverage) are correlated with reform, then analysts might incorrectly attribute insurance status differences to reform rather than to the unobservable factors, thereby biasing the estimated effects of interest.

Studies that focus on a particular state and use time series data (without controls for the time period) also suffer from a similar problem. Without adequate controls for economic and other changes over time, it is possible to attribute a change in insurance outcomes over time to reform when it is actually due to some other factor. Suppose, for example, that insurance markets became increasingly competitive, resulting in lower insurance prices and improved insurance coverage for reasons unrelated to reform. Without adequate controls for the changes in the insurance market, these effects could easily be attributed to reform measures. Unfortunately, it is easy to construct a wide array of such scenarios that would lead to biased estimates of the effects of reform. Finally, studies that control for time and state fixed effects may also provide biased estimates of reform. If, for reasons unrelated to reform, coverage improved over time (i.e., between the pre- and post-reform periods), then these effects would also be attributed to reform incorrectly.

Second-generation studies

Second-generation studies of reform were expressly designed to deal with the inherent weaknesses in the first generation of studies. In particular, the second generation of studies explicitly recognized that insurance trends in reform and non-reform states could vary for reasons other than reform. They also recognized that there might be systematic differences between reform and non-reform states.

During the 1990s, a popular way of estimating the effects of policies (and addressing the potential of biases) in the labor economics literature was reliance on approaches that treat the data as quasi-experimental (Meyer 1995; Hamermesh 2000). Unlike true experimental designs, where individuals are randomly assigned to a treatment or control group, the quasi-experimental approach treats the policy as the treatment and "assigns" individuals to the treatment group if they lived in a state that adopted the policy of interest. Individuals residing in other states without reforms are the control group for comparison. By focusing on changes in the outcome of interest before and after the policy was enacted for the treatment group relative to the control group, a measure of the effect of the policy can be ascertained.[5] This approach, commonly referred to as the difference-in-differences approach (DD) considers outcomes for four distinct groups: individuals in states that adopted the policy before and after its enactment (I_1 and I_2 respectively) and individuals in states that did not adopt the policy over the same two time periods (I_3 and I_4 respectively). In the context of small-group reform, this means that insurance outcomes, I_i, are observed for the groups shown in Figure 5.1. Unlike the first-generation studies, which essentially relied on obtaining the estimates

		Time period	
		Pre-reform	Post-reform
State type	Reform state	I_1	I_2
	Non-reform state	I_3	I_4

Figure 5.1 Description of difference-in-differences estimator.

of reform effects using cross-section data $(I_2 - I_4)$ or based on a time series for reform states $(I_2 - I_1)$, the quasi-experimental approach estimate is found by comparing time trends in insurance outcomes in reform versus non-reform states: $(I_2 - I_1) - (I_4 - I_3)$.

In essence, all the time trends common to both sets of states and all differences between states that are common in both time periods are "washed away." For example, if macroeconomic conditions worsened over time in all states, then this common effect would be differenced out because it would be reflected in both $(I_4 - I_3)$ and $(I_2 - I_1)$. Thus, the overall impact of reform is obtained by determining the change in the insurance outcome of interest in reform states over and above the change that occurred in other states.

While DD estimates control for time-invariant differences across states and state-invariant time trends, they do not account for the possibility that there could be differential factors affecting states over time. For example, if economic conditions worsened significantly more in non-reform states relative to reform states, causing insurance outcomes to worsen in the former states, then we might erroneously attribute the better outcomes in reform states to the effects of reform. Many of the second-generation studies address the possibility of differential time trends across states by using an additional control group – large firms or their employees – to account for this possibility.

By adding an additional control group, the estimate of reform now becomes a difference-in-differences-in-differences (DDD) estimator of the following form:

$$[(I_2 - I_1) - (I_4 - I_3)]_{\text{small firm}} - [(I_2 - I_1) - (I_4 - I_3)]_{\text{large firm}}$$

By subtracting out the DD estimates for large-firm employees, who are assumed to be unaffected by reform, the DDD estimates control for differential trends across reform and non-reform states that are common in both large and small firms. Using our example above, if economic conditions worsened in non-reform states relative to reform states (and for workers in all firm sizes), the difference would be removed from the final DDD estimate. Thus, the DDD estimate would no longer be contaminated by differential time trends across reform and non-reform states that are common to both small- and large-firm employees.

Studies that have relied on DD and DDD estimates of reform have generally found insignificant or small overall effects of reform. As noted above, however, the effects of reform may differ significantly for low-risk versus high-risk workers. Studies that have attempted to control for such differences (Simon 2002; Monheit and Schone 2004) have found some evidence that the impact of reform was relatively worse for low risks relative to high risks.

Methodological issues

How should one interpret the literature on small-group reform? While individual studies differ significantly in terms of their data and methodology, the overwhelming implication from the existing studies is that the effects of reform are relatively modest. As with most empirical studies, simplifying assumptions – both explicit and implicit – must be made to try to analyze the question of interest. The hope is that the assumptions have little impact on the estimated effects of reform. I have outlined several reasons why the first generation of studies may have produced biased estimates of the impact of reform. The question remains as to whether similar issues exist for the second generation of studies. In addition, there may be broader issues related to research design that need to be considered when evaluating all of the existing studies. To discuss these issues, I begin with empirical issues that apply to all studies of reform. Then, I focus on issues that pertain specifically to the latest studies. I conclude by discussing approaches that might be used in the future to improve our estimates of the effects of reform.

Methodological issues in designing studies of small-group reform

Existing studies of small-group reform use variation in the regulatory environment across states and across firms to identify the effects of reform. Designing such studies of small-group market reform requires that important assumptions be made about the nature of reform and the likely effects of reform on insurance outcomes. Many factors – such as the timing of the pre- and post-reform periods and the specification of the reforms – will affect the ability to detect a reform effect statistically.

Policy endogeneity

One maintained assumption in all studies of reform is that the reform policies that were adopted were exogenous. An extreme view of policy exogeneity is that purely random factors dictate whether individuals are either "assigned" to states that have adopted reforms or to those that have not, a condition clearly not met in the absence of a controlled experiment. A less extreme view is that state reform policies were adopted for reasons unrelated to the outcomes being studied (i.e., insurance outcomes). If this second assumption does not hold (i.e., states adopted reforms because of concerns about the insurance status of their citizens), then the assumption of policy exogeneity is not met and there is some potential for the estimated effects of policy to be biased.

Since policy, by design, is developed through a political process, there may be state-specific factors that influence the adoption of small-group reform. If there are observable factors that affect both the likelihood of adopting reforms and insurance coverage, then there may well be unobservable factors that have affected both as well, leading to biases in the estimates of reform on the insurance outcomes of interest. What do we know about the factors that influence the adoption of small-group reform? The only systematic study of the factors leading to reform is by Stream (1999). Stream uses pooled data on the states to determine the influence of a variety of variables on the extent of reform adopted. His outcome measure takes into account a number of different dimensions of reform: access (guaranteed renewability, guaranteed issue, portability, pre-existing condition limits), pricing (limits on rate increases, lower cost plans, affordability, and disclosure), rating restrictions, purchasing alliances and the definition of small groups. He uses each of these measures to create a summary statistic to reflect the extent of reform adopted (ranging from 0 to 10). He then regresses this summary variable on a variety of variables that he hypothesizes will affect reform: (1) the state's political context, (2) the fiscal health of the state, (3) the severity of the uninsured problem, (4) interest-group influence, (5) the regulatory environment in the state, and (6) the diffusion of regulations in neighboring states.[6] His findings indicate that the extent of reform increased with the severity of the problem of the uninsured, bureaucratic capacity, and the degree of reform diffusion (the stringency of the regulatory environment had a marginally significant effect on the degree of reform adopted).

It is unclear how important this potential endogeneity problem is for the literature on small-group reform. The findings of Stream indicate that there are clear determinants of small-group reform adoption. Stream's results may also provide some guidance for instrumenting the policy variable of interest since some factors that are correlated with reform adoption may be uncorrelated with insurance status (e.g., while this would be seem to be a more problematic issue for the first generation of studies, the ability of state and time fixed effects to solve the problem in the second generation of DD and DDD models becomes an empirical matter).

Besley and Case (2000) consider the issue of policy endogeneity in a different policy context by evaluating the impact of workers' compensation insurance on labor market outcomes. They argue that, with cross-sectional data, correlates of the policy variables should be included directly in the model of interest to get a more precise estimate of the policy effect.[7] In fact, they demonstrate that in the context of the problem they are investigating, the estimated policy effect is highly sensitive to the inclusion of state fixed effects and the choice of time-varying state variables. The sensitivity of their results raises similar concerns for early studies of small-group reform.[8] They note, however, that including such additional variables will never solve the problem completely since there are always omitted variables.

Beasley and Case also argue that their findings have important implications for DD and DDD studies. In particular, they raise concerns about the adequacy of the controls used in such studies. The fact that states may differ substantially in terms of the factors that lead them to adopt a policy may suggest that there are other important differences between control and treatment states, a point I discuss in more detail below. In sum, Beasley and Case suggest that if the goal is to understand the impact of a public policy, one needs to have a true understanding of the context in which the policy was adopted.

Policy timing and data

Another common feature of all studies of reform is the relatively short window used to study reform effects. Most studies of reform use data that span just slightly before reform was adopted to just slightly after its enactment. The issue of policy timing and the type of data used to evaluate reform raises several issues. First, policymakers are likely interested in the transition to reform as well as the longer-run effects of reform. To be able to distinguish between the transitory and permanent effects of reform, it is important to know how fast insurance markets adjust to the effects of reform. That is, should existing studies of reform be interpreted as long-run or short-run effects? While the existing body of research has roughly similar findings about the effects of reform, it remains important to evaluate reform over a longer period. The biggest impediment to doing this longer-run evaluation is the passage of time. On one hand, more time is needed to evaluate the longer-run effects of reform. On the other hand, as more time passes, there is a greater possibility that other factors change differentially across states, reducing the suitability of non-reform states as adequate controls.

Another important issue related to the study of small-group reform is the choice of the pre-reform time period. Most studies of reform that rely on observations pre- and post-reform choose the pre-reform period to be fairly close to the time during which reform was adopted. If insurers and other economic agents involved in insurance decisions were able to anticipate small-group reform regulations, it is possible that they may have responded to them prior to the enactment of reform. I know of no study that has analyzed the behavior of insurers and other economic agents just before reform relative to a period significantly before reform. To the extent that the behavior of agents was changed in anticipation of the regulations, it may be the case that the pre-reform time period already affects some of the impacts of reform. If such behavior exists, then this would bias estimates of reform toward not finding an impact, consistent with most of the existing literature.

Muticollinearity

As Table 5.1 indicates, reforms that were adopted across states were bundled; no state adopted a single reform measure. If the aim of research is to improve our understanding of the effects of reform, this bundling complicates matters. First, it may be very difficult to assess the effects of independent components of reform in analyses owing to multicollinearity (e.g., of the forty-four states that adopted guaranteed renewal, only one did not also adopt pre-existing condition restrictions). Thus, attempts at understanding which particular components of reform have an impact are going to be somewhat limited. As a consequence, many studies of reform, particularly the second generation of studies, focus on modeling reform based on its intensity (e.g., no reform, weak reform, stringent reform). In these cases, it remains difficult to assess the precise mechanisms through which reform might affect insurance coverage (and the possibility arises that specific components of reform may have offsetting effects, which cannot be identified in this manner).

Data quality

An additional issue that arises when evaluating studies of reform is data quality. The vast majority of studies of reform have relied on individual data; a much smaller group have used establishment-level data. One of the key predictions of the effects of reform is that they should have a differential effect depending on the riskiness of a firm. Studies that use individual data and try to assess the impact of reform differentially by risk (Monheit and Schone 2004; Simon 2002) use information on individual workers as a proxy for the riskiness of a firm. While this is a reasonable approach (and the only viable approach with these types of data), it does cause the level of firm riskiness to be measured with error. Establishment-level data overcome this problem to some extent, although they typically include only a small number of variables that are likely to represent the riskiness of the workforce (e.g., the age and sex distribution of workers).[9] These problems will generally be difficult to overcome in the absence of data that sample multiple workers in the same firms. Such data may greatly improve our understanding of the effects of small-market reforms.

Studies of small-group reform may also suffer to some extent from low statistical precision. For example, in the DDD studies the effects of reform are identified based on the sample of small-firm workers in reform states after the reform was adopted (and potentially for a subset of these workers if stratified by riskiness). The resulting sample size may, in fact, be quite small. While many of the estimates of small-group reform are modest, there are some point estimates that are sizable although statistically insignificant. As McCloskey and Ziliak (1996) note, it is important to consider the economic significance of point estimates, not just their statistical significance. More research, with larger samples as they become available, aimed at exploring the relatively large but statistically insignificant findings may provide insight as to whether these reported effects are statistical anomalies or whether they deserve more attention.

A final concern with many existing studies of small-group reform is that the standard errors of the main coefficients of interest may be reported as having more precision than they do in actuality. The main variables of interest are state-level reform indicators, which have much less variation than the micro-data imply. As a consequence, without adjustments of the standard errors to reflect the fact that state policy variables only vary over fifty states, the standard errors will be too small, and the effect of reform on insurance outcomes will be overstated (Moulton 1990).[10]

Methodological issues related to second-generation studies

The issues that were just raised indicate that there are important considerations that need to be taken into account when designing research to measure the effects of small-group reforms – issues that pertain to all of the existing studies. Given the methodological approach of the second generation of studies and the general interest in the economics literature in using quasi-experimental research designs, there are particular methodological issues that pertain to the second generation of studies.

Blundell and MacCurdy (1999) provide a detailed discussion of the difference-in-differences (DD) approach and argue that the formulation relies on fairly restrictive statistical assumptions. They note that two conditions need to be met in order for the DD estimates to be valid: (1) the passage of time must have a similar effect on treatment and control groups; and (2) the composition of treatment and control groups must be constant over time (prior to and after the policy change). The second generation of small-group reform studies has taken the first concern very seriously; the second issue has received far less attention.

It is precisely because there is concern that reform and non-reform states have had different experiences over the time period studied that researchers relied on difference-in-differences-in-differences (DDD) estimators. By adding large-firm workers as an additional control group, the effect of differential experiences over time in reform and non-reform states is removed from the reform estimate (as long as the differential time effects also affected large-firm employees in a similar fashion). Whether the use of large-establishment workers as an additional control group improves the estimates is dependent on whether large-establishment employees serve as good controls. I address this issue below.

The condition that the composition of the treatment and control groups be constant (i.e., that the characteristics of workers in small and large firms – both observable and unobservable – remain similar over time) has received far less attention in the literature. In essence, the issue is whether there is nonrandom selection of employees into small firms that differs across reform and non-reform states over time. There are reasons to think that the characteristics of workers may have changed differentially since there have been changes in the general labor force. In 1990, Hispanic workers represented 7.1 percent of all workers; in 1999, they represented 8.6 percent of all workers (*US Statistical Abstract* 2001). Over the same time period, female labor force participation rates increased from 57.5 percent to 60 percent (*US Statistical Abstract* 2001). While these changes appear modest, they are an indication that the structure of labor markets and the distribution of workers across firms may have changed over the time period. In fact, if small-group reforms were effective, then the possibility arises that workers may have re-sorted themselves across firms, finding small firms more attractive than they were previously. Little work has been done to evaluate these trends systematically in the context of small-group reforms.

A final issue related to treatment and control groups is whether the groups unaffected by the policy change represent good controls. In the context of the literature on small-group reforms, this issue seems particularly problematic with respect to large-firm employees. There are several issues. First, large-firm employees may be significantly different in terms of their experiences. In particular, large firms may be somewhat insulated from economic fluctuations. Variation in insurance offers for employees over the 1996–2001 period by establishment size suggest this to be the case. For firms with 1,000 or more employees, offer rates varied from a low of 97.6 percent to a high of 99.8 percent over this time period. (Similarly in firms with 100–999 employees, offer rates ranged from 95.9 percent to 97.6 percent.) In contrast, in firms with less than fifty employees there was somewhat more variation (from a low of 62.3 percent to a high of 67.8 percent).[11] The relatively high offer rates of large firms and their low variation indicate that large firms may not be sensitive to other factors that may affect insurance status beyond the reforms. The potential lack of sensitivity of large-firm offer rates suggests that large firms may not be an effective additional control group, since they may not be affected by exogenous changes in the same way as small firms. For example, if bad economic conditions lead to greater reductions in insurance coverage in small firms and if economic conditions became worse in reform states, then the DDD estimates would attribute this change to reform inappropriately. Another possible explanation for these differences in offer rate sensitivity over time may be that tastes for insurance of individuals is correlated with firm size (i.e., workers with a strong taste for coverage choose to work in large firms that are more inclined to offer coverage).[12] It would appear hard to argue that selection of workers into firms by size is random.

Finally, another requirement in using large-firm employees as an additional control group is that they are unaffected by small-group reforms.

Small-group reforms were clearly designed to address flaws in the small-group market. It is well known, however, that public policies typically have general equilibrium effects. Since insurers generally provide coverage to both large and small groups, it may be the case that insurers somehow adjusted their behavior and offerings to large groups as a consequence of new requirements to serve the small-group market. If such general equilibrium effects exist, then estimates of the effects of reform derived from DDD estimates will potentially be biased (although the direction of the bias is unclear).[13] Moreover, it is also possible that large firms may have responded to reform measures by changing the generosity of their coverage. For example, if a large firm had many employees who were married to workers in small firms, then large firms may have tried to shift coverage towards these small firms after the adoption of reform. For all of these reasons, large firms may not serve as an adequate control group that was not affected by reform.

Econometric issues related to the second-generation studies

Given the popularity of using quasi-experimental approaches to analyze policy, there has been a growing literature that has focused on analyzing and improving the estimates and techniques to make them more general and more robust. While the new literature has not yet been applied to analyzing the impacts of small-group reform, it does suggest that many of the techniques could be used to improve the quality of existing estimates.

One theme that has received attention in the methodological literature is the stringent requirements associated with DD estimators.[14] Abadie (2002) proposes a semi-parametric technique that relaxes the assumption that the treatments and controls would have faced similar circumstances in the absence of the policy. In particular, his semi-parametric approach explicitly accounts for the possibility that treatments and controls differ systematically. His approach also provides estimates of the effect of the treatment that varies by observable variables. Such an approach might be fruitful in understanding the distributional consequences of small-group reform policies for population subgroups.

Athey and Imbens (2002) also propose an alternative formulation to DD referred to as the changes-in-changes model. They explicitly recognize that policies have the potential to affect the entire distribution of outcomes, rather than just mean outcomes. Moreover, they acknowledge that there may be policy interest in understanding the entire distribution of changes that result from the policy. They argue that the DD estimates are very sensitive to the statistical assumptions required for the model; their more general approach recognizes that both observables and unobservables can vary over time and may provide a more meaningful measure of the effects of policy.[15] Even with the advantages of their approach, they maintain the assumption that treatment and control groups remain stable over time. Their work further demonstrates the restrictive set of assumptions required for DD estimation. For the purposes of evaluating the effects of small-group reform, there may be gains by estimating models with less restrictive assumptions.

Further steps for the third generation of studies

There are many directions for future research on the effects of small-group reforms. While existing estimates paint a fairly consistent picture that reform had relatively modest effects, the issues noted above suggest that such estimates could be improved. As methodological advances are made, it will be interesting to see if the general set of results hold. In addition, the assessment of reform has focused on a fairly specific set of outcomes. There may be other outcomes that are potentially affected by reform that are of policy interest. In this section, I outline potential directions for future research.

An important step for future research is to expand our understanding of the effects of reform along several new dimensions. For example, there is serious interest in gaining insight into the nature of family decision making regarding health insurance choices. Greater insight into family behavior may be gained by studying small-group reforms. Since health insurance decisions are often family decisions, it is possible that spouses of small-firm workers might be affected by small-group reforms. Analyses that focus on the effects of small-group reforms on families rather than individual workers may provide further insight into health insurance decisions within families and the tradeoffs that are made across family members in obtaining coverage. The findings may also reveal that reforms had indirect effects on individuals not employed in small firms.

In addition to analyzing families, little is known about the effects of small-group reforms on health outcomes and health behaviors. While most of the existing literature indicates a relatively small overall effect of reform, there are studies that find that reform has consequences on insurance coverage for population subgroups. Little is known as to whether these effects have translated into improved health care access and healthy behaviors for those who benefited from the reforms or whether those who were harmed also faced changes in health care access and health care use. Since insurance is viewed primarily as a vehicle for obtaining access to health care, it would be informative to see if reform had any impact on these measures.

Finally, the existing evidence indicates that the effects of reform varied across the population (e.g., high- versus low-risk workers). The findings suggest that much remains to be learned about the distributional consequences of reform. Recent methodological advances that have focused on the effects of policies over the population, rather than just mean effects, could be applied to small-group reforms. Such information will potentially be useful to policymakers because it will provide information about winners and losers from reform.[16]

Conclusions

In this chapter, I have presented a critical assessment of the methods used in the existing literature on small-group market reforms. Overall, the literature paints a fairly consistent picture that reform had modest effects overall on insurance outcomes, with some evidence that high-risk workers gained at the expense of low-risk workers. While the existing studies are not definitive and can be improved, they do suggest that a body of evidence is building about the overall effects of reform. There is simply no strong evidence that reform had profound effects on the small-group health insurance market.

The existing literature on small-group market reforms also indicates that there has been clear progress in the methodological rigor of existing studies. The second generation of studies provides the best existing estimates of the effects of reform. As methodology continues to improve, these estimates can be refined further and the robustness of the results to weaker statistical assumptions can be ascertained.

As researchers have started to explore in other contexts, it is also possible that small-group reforms had effects on outcomes other than insurance status. Understanding more general effects of these reform measures on outcomes related to labor markets, family decision making regarding health insurance, health care use and health care access, and health outcomes will broaden our understanding of the role of insurance market reforms. Such information is crucial for effectively designing efficient policies that are aimed at improving health care coverage and health care access for workers.

Acknowledgments

The views in this chapter are my own. No official endorsement by the Agency for Healthcare Research and Quality or the Department of Health and Human Services is intended or should be inferred. I thank Lindsay Harris for research assistance and Alan Monheit for very helpful comments.

Notes

1 For example, premiums may vary by 20 percent above and below a "typical" premium. As Hall (2000/2001) notes, a "typical" premium may not be the premium charged to an average-risk firm. Hall asserts that insurers may price most risks at the low end of the rating band, with the worst risks at the top of the band.

2 Apart from restricting the rate of growth of premiums from year to year, small-group reform regulation did not regulate average premiums.

3 Clearly, the effect will depend on the degree to which premiums are compressed. If premiums are not compressed significantly and if high-risk firms are not sensitive to the access measures, then the overall effects of reform might be quite small.
4 Hing and Jensen (1999) is an exception. Their study relies on cross-sectional establishment data from 1994.
5 If there is measurement error in the assignment of individuals to the treatment or control group, then there well be a bias in favor of not finding an effect of the policy. For example, such error in assignment might occur if an individual lives in a non-reform state (i.e., classified as being in the control group) but works in a neighboring state that adopted reform (i.e., the individual is actually in the treatment group).
6 Specifically Stream argued that: (1) greater Republican influence will make a state more predisposed to aiding small businesses (political context); (2) reform is easier to undertake in a healthy fiscal environment (fiscal health); (3) the greater the problem with the uninsured, the more likely for reform to occur (problem severity); (4) a greater proportion of health care industry workers will increase the likelihood of reform while a larger proportion of insurance industry workers should reduce its likelihood (interest group influence); (5) a large regulatory bureaucracy should increase reforms, as should a more stringent regulatory environment (regulatory environment); and (6) reforms are more likely to be adopted if neighboring states have already done so (diffusion).
7 Suppose, for example, that the proportion of women in the population increases the likelihood of adopting small-market reforms and is positively associated with insurance coverage. Omitting this variable from the analysis will lead to the policy variable providing an overestimate of the effect of the policy on insurance coverage.
8 Kubik and Moran (2003) also address policy endogeneity concerns in the context of analyzing state excise taxes on cigarettes. They find evidence that state taxes are endogenous by showing that price elasticity estimates of the demand for cigarettes are sensitive to instrumenting for these policies (using the timing of state elections as an instrument).
9 A further weakness of establishment-level data is that limited information is available on factors that are likely to affect insurance coverage decisions by both employers and their employees.
10 This problem may not be especially severe in the context of small-group reform, since the estimated effects of reform have generally been small and many have not been statistically significant. Zuckerman and Rajan (1999) address this concern by estimating the effects of reform on state-level aggregates.
11 These figures are derived from Health Insurance Component Analytical Tool (MEPSnet/IC).
12 See Monheit and Vistnes (1999) for evidence of sorting of workers across firms by preferences for insurance.
13 One way to address this concern would be to calculate DDD estimates on large firms, using a sample of large-firm employees from time periods prior to reform and large-firm employees over time periods that straddle the reform measures to see if there were systematic changes in coverage for these employees over time.
14 Most of the literature aimed at improving quasi-experimental estimates focus on DD models, rather than DDD models.
15 Since their approach allows for differences in both observables and unobservables, they are able to address the issue of policy endogeneity since unobservables can be different across treatment and control groups.

16 Distributional effects have been found to be important in other contexts. Bitler *et al.* (2003) find that one particular welfare program experiment has very different effects on earnings throughout the income distribution.

References

Abadie, A. (2002) "Semiparametric Difference-in-difference Estimators." Working paper, Cambridge, MA: Harvard University.

Athey, S. and Imbens, G. (2002) "Identification and Inference in Nonlinear Difference-in-Difference Models." Working paper 280, Cambridge, MA: National Bureau of Economic Research.

Besley, T. and Case, A. (2000) "Unnatural Experiments? Estimating the Incidence of Endogenous Policies." *Economic Journal*, 110: F672–F694.

Bitler, M., Gelbach, J., and Hoynes, H. (2003) "What Mean Impacts Miss: Distributional Effects of Welfare Reform Experiments." Working paper, Davis, CA: University of California at Davis.

Blundell, R. and MacCurdy, T. (1999) "Labor Supply: A Review of Alternative Approaches" in A. Aschenfelter and D. Card (eds), *Handbook of Labor Economics*, pp. 1569–1695.

Buchmueller, T. and DiNardo, J. (2002) "Did Community Rating Induce an Adverse Selection Death Spiral? Evidence from New York, Pennsylvania, and Connecticut." *American Economic Review*, 92 (1): 280–294.

Buchmueller, T. and Jensen, G. (1997) "Small Group Reform in a Competitive Managed Care Market: The Case of California, 1993 to 1995." *Inquiry*, 34 (3): 249–263.

Hall, M. (2001/2002) "The Structure and Enforcement of Health Insurance Rating Reforms." *Inquiry*, 37 (4): 376–388.

Hamermesh, D. (2000) "The Craft of Labormetrics." *Industrial and Labor Relations Review*, 53 (3): 363–380.

Health Insurance Component Analytical Tool (MEPSnet/IC) (2003) Rockville, MD: Agency for Healthcare Research and Quality.

Hing, E. and Jensen, G. (1999) "Health Insurance Portability and Accountability Act of 1996: Lessons from the States." *Medical Care*, 37 (7): 692–705.

Jensen, G. and Morrisey, M. (1999) "Small Group Reform and Insurance Provision by Small Firms, 1989–1995." *Inquiry*, 36 (2): 176–187.

Kaestner, R. and Simon, K. (2002) "Labor Market Consequences of State Health Insurance Regulation." *Industrial and Labor Relations Review*, 56 (1): 136–159.

Kubik, J. and Moran, J. (2003) "Can Policy Changes be Treated as Natural Experiments? Evidence from Cigarette Excise Taxes." Working paper, Syracuse, NY: Syracuse University.

Marquis, S. and Long, S. (2001/2002) "Effects of 'Second Generation' Small Group Health Insurance Market Reforms, 1993 to 1997." *Inquiry*, 38 (4): 365–380.

McCloskey, D. and Ziliak, S. (1996) "The Standard Error of Regression." *Journal of Economic Literature*, March: 97–114.

Meyer, B.D. (1995) "Natural and Quasi-experiments in Economics." *Journal of Business and Economic Statistics*, 13 (2): 151–161.

Monheit, A. and Schone, B. (2004) "How Has Small Group Market Reform

Affected Employee Health Insurance Coverage?" *Journal of Public Economics*, 88 (1–2): 237–254.

Monheit, A. and Vistnes, J. (1999) "Health Insurance Availability at the Workplace." *Journal of Human Resources*, 34 (4): 770–785.

Moulton, B. (1990) "An Illustration of a Pitfall in Estimating the Effects of Aggregate Variables on Micro Units." *Review of Economics and Statistics*, 72 (2): 334–338.

Simon, K.I. (2000) "The Impact of Small-Group Health Insurance Reform on the Price and Availability of Health Benefits." Working paper, Ithaca, NY: Cornell University.

Simon, K.I. (2002) "Did Small-group Health Insurance Reforms Work?" Working paper, Ithaca, NY: Cornell University.

Sloan, F. and Conover, C. (1998) "Effects of State Reforms on Health Insurance Coverage of Adults." *Inquiry*, 35 (3): 280–293.

Statistical Abstract of the United States 2001 (2001) Washington, DC: US Bureau of the Census.

Stream, C. (1999) "Health Reform in the United States: A Model of State Small Group Health Insurance Market Reforms." *Political Research Quarterly*, 52 (3): 499–525.

Zuckerman, S. and Rajan, S. (1999) "An Alternative Approach to Measuring the Effects of Insurance Market Reforms." *Inquiry*, 36 (1): 44–56.

Part III

Perspectives from the field

How can access to affordable coverage be sustained?

6 An insurance executive reflects on health insurance market reform

Sanford B. Herman

The nature of American society and its stress on voluntary action by its citizenry has, in many ways, resulted in a significant disconnect between the concepts of accessibility to and affordability of health care coverage. Anything related to universal coverage, on the other hand, has had the connotation of a mandate or forced action – something generally to be avoided.

The general precepts of group insurance revolve around the law of large numbers and the fact that if you get a broad cross-section of a working population you can achieve reasonable cost results. That all worked well back in the 1950s and 1960s for the large-employer market, where the offering of medical insurance benefits was the overwhelming norm, and employer subsidies were sufficiently generous to ensure virtually universal participation by their employees. Much of this situation was related to the prevalence of collective bargaining within such industries or, in some cases, the mere threat of potential unionization. Large industrial America, as we knew it back then, was the closest thing that America has had to universal health care coverage.

This somewhat ideal model never quite fit the small-employer or individual market because of the very voluntary nature of American society. Small employers were not forced by either the government or the competitive marketplace (including labor unions) to make coverage available for their employees, and when they did, the level of subsidy was often not sufficient to assure the broadest possible employee participation. The individual insurance marketplace was, and continues to be, completely voluntary. As such, small employers and individuals could pick the time and place to enter the insurance market. Faced with these examples of potential adverse selection, insurance carriers desiring to offer affordable coverage felt the necessity to utilize various forms of underwriting. Freedom, combined with relative affordability, came with a price – that being the selection of risks – which, unfortunately, was a barrier to accessibility for a certain segment of the population.

These somewhat optimal cost-containing models – fairly universal coverage in the large-employer market and underwritten coverage in the small-employer and individual markets – worked for a while. However, a deteriorating economy combined with hyperinflation in the 1970s caused employers and insurers to take actions to contain some of the escalating costs. These included self-insurance mechanisms for larger groups that helped avoid costly state mandates, premium taxes and insurer risk charges, and plan design changes within all of the markets. We also began to see the emergence and modest growth of the various forms of managed health care in both the smaller-group and large-group marketplaces. Additionally, some insurers seeking to obtain cost advantages sought to utilize various new underwriting techniques such as tier and durational rating, re-entry underwriting, along with the experience rating of small groups. It wasn't good enough to underwrite up-front and then fully pool the inforce risks. Some carriers had to continually "cleanse" their pool populations. These were the abuses that led to the initial small-group rating reforms in the late 1980s and the more comprehensive small-group and individual market reforms of the early to mid-1990s.

Rationale for reform

The major rationale for the small-group and individual market reforms during the 1990s centered on accessibility – addressing the real and perceived abuses of the insurance industry. It was felt that if only all citizens could have complete access to insurance coverage at the prevailing price level, this would make a great dent in the uninsured population that around that time numbered approximately 37 million. What the reformers failed to take into account, either intentionally or unintentionally, was that while the anecdotal stories made great newspaper headlines, these examples represented only a small fraction of the uninsured population, many of whom were within families having at least one worker. Many were unable to afford coverage, and in actuality the various forms of rate compression adopted by state small-group reform left many of these younger and healthier uninsureds even less willing and/or able to pay for coverage.

Market change

If anything, small-group and individual market reforms, combined with the continued overall escalation in medical care costs (which impacted large employers and governmental entities as well), hastened the rise of managed care carriers and the decline of indemnity insurers. The HMOs were able to put into place immediate fixes in the form of utilization controls and deep provider discounts, that more than offset the incremental costs of the reform legislation. With the decline in indemnity insurance, we also saw a major reduction in the number of significant health insurance players. Since the cost of establishing local and national provider networks is quite prohibitive, many of the former players merged, while others dropped out of the business either officially or on a *de facto* basis. This development can be illustrated by what transpired in New Jersey in just a few years. As of 1995, shortly after the New Jersey Small Employer Health Insurance Program (SEHBP) and Individual Health Coverage Program (IHCP) were enacted and implemented, there were fourteen separate insurance entities in the small-employer market having at least 2 percent of the market. By 2001 that number had dropped to eight, and many of these carriers were quite new. It is not clear at this time whether the concentration of market share will result in downward or upward pressure on bottom-line medical insurance premium costs.

Throughout the remainder of the decade following the state reform legislative activity, the United States enjoyed one of the longest and strongest periods of economic growth. However, we barely made a dent in reducing the size of the uninsured population. Additionally, by the end of this economic expansion, most of the HMOs had hit a brick wall relative to their ability to further reduce claim costs and, with the prolonged current period of economic difficulties, we now have millions more who are on the uninsured rolls.

State reform, as well as the limited federal action in the form of the Health Insurance Portability and Accountability Act (HIPAA) of 1996, have had little success in reducing the number of uninsured persons. The primary reason for this lack of success is that the reforms have not effectively addressed the underlying economic reality that many employers and their employees are either unable or unwilling to pay for such coverage, and little is going to change this in the absence of a governmental mandate.

An alternative approach

In order to address the lack of health insurance in the United States, we must come to grips with the fundamental conflicts and contradictions within American society regarding medical care. We have an insatiable appetite for consuming medical care but no desire to pay for what we want to consume. We tout freedom of choice and action, but we will not accept a system that forces the consequences for making a wrong choice. We expect near miracles from our medical care system, but use our litigious nature to undermine the providers. Additionally, we don't want to pay directly for universal health care coverage, but are willing to pay for it back-door by accepting professional fees and hospital charges which are loaded for such things as uncompensated care and bad debt. Most important, we have a political system that does not permit elected officials to make the hard and unpopular decisions.

Unfortunately, the spur to voluntarism sought by insurance market reform has not materialized. Consequently, we should seriously consider a nationally mandated benefit plan which would be funded by a combination of employer and employee contributions, along with an individual mandate containing subsidies varying by income level. For small employers, there would be some phase-in general revenue support as well to limit their out-of-pocket expenses. This program would be best served by a competitive private marketplace, acting within the parameters of reasonable regulation, as opposed to the establishment of a massive governmental bureaucracy.

There are some significant precedents for such a mandatory approach to universal coverage. One example is the system of workers' compensation programs which resulted from state legislation during the first half of the twentieth century. These programs generally involve the private insurance market, although in a small number of states an exclusive state fund is utilized. Another example is mandated automobile insurance that also arose at the state level. Unemployment insurance arose as a federal mandate during the late 1930s, although the bulk of the responsibility for administering and funding these programs was left to the states. Finally, while not private sector programs, Social Security and Medicare are other insurance programs arising from federal mandates.

As part of such a comprehensive solution, we will need to enact national medical malpractice reform. One element of this would be an adjunct judicial system made up of expert panels that could look at such cases. Experts would make objective decisions as to the merit of malpractice claims and, where there was fault, make a reasonable evaluation regarding appropriate damage awards. Such a panel would also need to have the authority to deal with the professional licenses of blatant or repeat offenders. In this way, we could cut down on many of the unnecessary and costly procedures and tests done or ordered by the physician community, while still protecting the rights of patients to quality care.

It would also be appropriate to put in certain controls on prescription drug prices. From an equity perspective, it is hard to understand why Americans subsidize the drug costs of other nations while facing excessive prices for prescription drugs at home.

Finally, we would need to have at least some portion of the managed care elements in such a health care plan in order to keep costs down. This would probably not look quite like Canada, which has a degree of rationing, but would be a bit more tightly managed than the advocates of a federal Patients' Bill of Rights would have it. Such a system of managed care controls would, however, need to have adequate protections, such as timely external appeals. From the perspective of premium rating, something akin to community rating, with a program of risk adjustment allowances, would be appropriate under a system of universal coverage.

Conclusions

To sum up, implementation of regulatory reform in the small-group and individual health insurance markets does not appear to have effectively spurred the kind of voluntary response by employers and individuals that would significantly reduce the size of the uninsured population. With accelerating health care costs and double-digit increases in health insurance premiums, it is likely that only a more direct and mandatory approach will be able to address the underlying reasons for the lack of coverage among millions of individuals and families.

7 An insurance commissioner reflects on insurance market reform

Steven B. Larsen

I want to comment on health insurance market reform by drawing upon my experience as insurance commissioner for the state of Maryland. Reform in the small-group and individual markets was implemented in Maryland in 1993 and is generally considered to be successful. However, given the growth in health care costs and health insurance premiums, there has been much pressure to make basic changes to reform and I will discuss this issue below. I want to begin my remarks by focusing on some specific features of reform and some basic data which I think support the notion that reform, at least in the small-group market, has been successful.

Small-group reform

Small-group reform in Maryland applies to public or private employers with two to fifty eligible employees or to self-employed individuals and is based upon a standard health insurance plan developed by an independent commission. Under state law, the Maryland Health Care Commission develops a comprehensive standard health benefit plan that is exempt from all mandated benefits passed by the legislature. However, as a practical matter, the commission is under intense political pressure to incorporate these benefits in the plan. Consequently, in almost all cases, benefits included in the standard plan tend to track what has been mandated. As a recent example, the legislature passed a mandate to cover morbid obesity and the commission declined to add this to the benefit package. Literally a few days later, the commission's executive director was summoned to explain this action to the state legislature. Thus, while it may appear as though reform is exempt from adding such benefit mandates, in reality that is not the case. There is constant political pressure and tradeoffs that arise in defining the benefit package.

Affordability cap

I also want to note that a key feature of small-group reform in Maryland is an affordability cap. This provision is a backdoor way of forcing the commission to look at the level of mandated benefits in standard plans every year. The affordability cap requires the average annual premium for standard plans not to exceed 12 percent of the annual average wage in the state of Maryland. If premiums exceed the 12 percent cap, in theory, the commission is supposed to re-evaluate the benefit package and decide on what type of benefits to cut back. So far, Maryland has been successful in keeping premiums below 12 percent of average annual wages. Typically, the way the commission has met this constraint is to progressively increase deductibles. For example, Maryland has a $1,000 deductible for individuals and a $2,000 deductible for the family coverage (for PPO coverage) compared to levels of $500 and $750, respectively, when reform was first implemented. Premiums are also subject to rating bands of ±40 percent and are subject to modified community rating based on age and geography. (Health status cannot be considered.) Small-group reform in Maryland also imposes a minimum loss ratio of 75 percent, and the insurance commissioner has the ability to deny rate increases if a health plan consistently falls below the 75 percent requirement. However, this provision has been invoked only once in the last ten years.

Premiums and availability of coverage

When data that does not adjust for differences in benefit packages are examined, Maryland has average premiums that exceed the national average for firms with less than fifty employees. For example, 1999 data from the Medical Expenditure Panel Survey (MEPS) indicate that small employer premiums for family and individual coverage in Maryland were $6,785 and $2,735, respectively, compared to $6,062 and $2,475 nationally, or 11.9 percent and 10.3 percent higher. MEPS data also indicate that Maryland's premiums exceed those of a number of other states with rate regulations that were either more relaxed or more stringent than those of Maryland (Wicks 2002: 1, 18–20).[1] However, when premium data for a standard benefit package are examined across these states (obtained from the National Association of Insurance Underwriters for a hypothetical group of ten employees of different ages and health conditions), Maryland's rates are 9 percent below the average for these states (Wicks 2002: 20).

Maryland has also seen an increase in the number of small businesses offering coverage and this has been viewed as one measure of success. For example, based on 1999 data, 57 percent of small businesses offered coverage in Maryland, exceeding the national average of 47 percent. Of particular interest are small groups of less than ten who are especially sensitive to increases in premiums. For these small groups, 51 percent offered coverage in Maryland compared to only 39 percent nationally. Finally, as a result of the types of political pressure noted above, Maryland's standard plan is more generous than most of the small-group policies that are available.

Challenges to small-group reform

What are the issues confronting small-group reform today? Like every other state, rising health care costs are creating critical barriers to affordable coverage in the small-group market. From the period of 1996 to 1999, there was about a 25 percent increase in premiums in Maryland, but the state is hoping to hold rate increases to between 12 percent to 20 percent. Even without premium inflation, as soon as someone enters a new age rating band they have a rate increase of almost 20 percent. Some individuals experience premium increases of 40 percent when all the rating factors come together the wrong way. One response by the legislature has been to reduce the 12 percent affordability cap (which has been in place for ten years) to 10 percent rather than changing the scope of benefits in the standard benefit package. Adjusting the affordability cap is also a way to make the commission revisit the costs associated with the inclusion of mandated and other benefit provisions, as well as the design of the standard health plan.

In Maryland, employers have to offer their employees the standard benefit package but can purchase a rider to enhance the benefit package and reduce out-of-pocket costs such as deductibles. However, by doing so, the rider will also add to small-employer premiums. Although carriers can sell more policies with a rider, the inclusion of a rider reflects the tension that individuals want broad coverage but do not want to pay much out of pocket for the associated services. This experience suggests that, from an employer's perspective, it is important to offer more complete coverage, either first-dollar coverage or something that approximates a more comprehensive set of benefits, even if it costs more, rather than having relatively high deductibles which may generate complaints from their employees.

The small-group market in Maryland has also seen the number of insured lives consistently increase over the last ten years. Only most recently has there been a slight dip in enrollment, so, overall, reform has been viewed as relatively successful. The state plans to use the affordability cap as a way to contain costs which is likely to require some diminution in the level of benefits. The state health care commission will be responsible for implementing these changes.

Finally, a series of interviews with state regulators, representatives of health plans, and insurance agents and brokers revealed considerable agreement that small-group reform has been beneficial to small employers and has made coverage more readily available and affordable for high-risk groups. Moreover, no one interviewed attributed the rapid rise in small-group premiums in Maryland to the implementation of reform (Wicks 2002: 2).

Reform in the individual insurance market

The experience of the individual health insurance market in Maryland is in stark contrast to that of the small-group market. There has not been any change to existing reform provisions such as guaranteed issue, modified community rating, or restrictions on underwriting. Like many states, Maryland has one large carrier, a non-profit Blue Cross Blue Shield plan representing 80 percent of the individual market. (Kaiser Permanente is next with just 7 percent of the market.) Thus, in reality, the state has one carrier and then a handful of carriers with a single-digit market share, and then around twenty carriers that have less than 100 people insured. As a result, it's a very concentrated market.

As with the small-group market, Maryland's individual market has been experiencing large premium increases for 2001–2003 on the order of 12 percent to 20 percent. Carriers are becoming more aggressive in their use of age rating bands, which are not restricted in the individual market. As a result, large premium variation can occur between cohorts of ages 20–25 and 60–64. One of the things that Maryland is beginning to focus on is the limitation on coverage due to medical underwriting. This appears to be a growing problem in the individual market where the combination of rate increases, stricter underwriting, and higher incidence of exclusionary riders drive market enrollment.

As a way to take the pressure off the individual market, Maryland instituted a high-risk pool, the Maryland Health Insurance Plan (MHIP), effective July 1, 2003. It is funded through hospital assessments, using Maryland's hospital rate-setting system (the only one in the country) rather than just assessing all the carriers. There were about 7,000 people in the prior high-risk pooling mechanism, the Substantial, Available, and Affordable Coverage Program (SAAC), an initiative which provided carriers who offer open-enrollment to high-risk individuals in their individual products with discounted hospital rates. With funding for the new MHIP, we will have the capacity to triple enrollment. The 2002 Trade Adjustment Assistance Reform Act will also provide some Marylanders whose jobs have been displaced by trade with tax credits for health insurance.

Conclusions

Has reform had an impact on the number of uninsured in Maryland? Unfortunately, it is difficult to discern any correlation, let alone causality, between market reform and changes in uninsured rates. For example, even with very progressive and effective small-group reform (and individual reform that has been less effective), Maryland has about 13 percent of its population, or 700,000 individuals, uninsured. Small-group reform has been viewed as improving access to coverage among employees of small firms as the number of small businesses offering coverage has increased in the years following reform implementation. However, the state faces an ongoing challenge to ensure that such access will be possible at affordable premiums.

Note

1 Comparison states included New Jersey, Delaware, Virginia, North Carolina, Florida, and Colorado. Maryland and New Jersey are viewed as having tight rating restrictions. Florida and Colorado are similar to Maryland in not permitting premiums to be adjusted on the basis of health status, while Delaware and Virginia have very lenient rating restrictions compared to Maryland.

Reference

Wicks, E.K. (2002) "Assessment of the Performance of Small-Group Health Insurance Market Reforms in Maryland." Naples, FL: Health Management Associates, 19 February.

8 Can access to affordable individual health insurance be sustained?

Karen Pollitz

The answer to the question posed in the title is uncertain. Nowhere in the United States is affordable and sustainable coverage a hallmark of individual health insurance. To the contrary, the individual market suffers from many inherent weaknesses. It is small, voluntary, expensive, and unsubsidized; it experiences high rates of turnover; and it is vulnerable to adverse selection. In every state, individual coverage is affordable and accessible only for some. In theory, this market could work well for everyone. However, sweeping structural change would be required to make coverage mandatory (or otherwise universal) and much more heavily subsidized than it is today.

Absent such sweeping change, policymakers must face the reality that this market will never be able to well serve all who need it. Incremental regulation to solve some problems will likely exacerbate others. There will always be winners and losers. Ultimately, balancing these tradeoffs is a political question. Policymakers will need to decide the mix of winners and losers they can best abide.

Individual market reform in a national context

Ideally, health insurance in any market or program would meet three simultaneous goals for all people all of the time: coverage should be accessible, affordable, and adequate to meet health care needs. Because states cannot satisfy all three objectives for all their citizens in today's unhealthy individual market, they have followed different paths to doing the best they can. States have adopted a variety of regulatory approaches – from the comprehensive protections required in New Jersey to *laissez-faire* in other states – in order to promote affordable coverage. Regardless of approach, though, tradeoffs are required.

Focusing on New Jersey's comprehensive reform, all individual health policies must be sold on a guaranteed issue basis to all residents all of the time. Everyone who needs individual health insurance – those who are self-employed, retired, or working in jobs without benefits – must be offered the chance to buy it. All policies must provide for a standardized, comprehensive set of covered benefits. These include hospital and physician care, maternity care, mental health care, and prescription drugs. Preexisting condition exclusions are limited and credit must be given for prior coverage, allowing people to change policies without penalty as long as they remain continuously covered. Finally, all individual health insurance premiums must be based on community rating, with no adjustments for age, gender, or geography.

Under these rules, individual coverage in New Jersey is not inexpensive. A typical HMO policy with a $30 office visit co-pay costs almost $400 per month per person.[1] Considering that national *per capita* health care spending now exceeds $5,000 per year, this price is not extraordinary (Levitt *et al.* 2003). Even so, residents with modest incomes are hard pressed to buy coverage at these rates.

By contrast, in most other states, New Jersey-like insurance regulations do not apply in the individual market. Without guaranteed issue protections, consumers in other states can be and are turned down based on health status. Where a comprehensive benefit standard is not required, coverage for some key health services (maternity, mental health care, and prescription drugs) is often limited. Where community rating does not apply, insurance premiums can vary enormously based on age, health status, and other factors. Age rating, alone, causes premiums to vary by as much as 6:1. Premium surcharges for health factors can add hundreds, often thousands, of dollars to the annual cost of coverage. Furthermore, consumers face considerable uncertainty when shopping for individual health insurance. It is impossible to know whether one might be turned down, charged more, or offered substandard coverage based on a current or past medical condition.

Pollitz *et al.* (2001) tested medical underwriting practices in eight individual health insurance markets (in Arizona, California, Florida, Illinois, Indiana, Iowa, Texas, and Virginia) and illustrated the degree of uncertainty consumers face. People in less than perfect health rarely obtained "clean offers" of coverage from insurers – that is, they usually could not buy the policy they wanted for the insurer's advertised standard rate. Instead, even minor health conditions, such as hay fever or mild depression, triggered denials or "substandard" offers (such as premium surcharges or riders eliminating coverage for certain benefits, conditions, or body parts and systems). Obtaining coverage was even more difficult for applicants with more serious health conditions (asthma, high blood pressure) and impossible for an applicant with HIV. (See Table 8.1.) Furthermore, wide-ranging premiums were quoted for similar coverage to applicants with different ages and health conditions. In Illinois, for example, one carrier offered the same policy to a 24-year-old woman with hay fever for $183 per month and to a 64-year-old man with hypertension for $1,764 per month.

In Pollitz *et al.* (2001), consumers also applied for health insurance in

Table 8.1 Underwriting actions taken on sixty applications for individual coverage by persons with various health conditions

Underwriting action condition	*"Clean offers"*	*"Substandard offers"*	*"Denials"*
Hay fever	3	52	5
Knee injury (repaired ten years ago)	15	38	7
Asthma	3	49	9
Breast cancer (treated seven years ago)	11	23	26
Depression	9	37	14
Hypertension/overweight	2	25	33
HIV	0	0	60

Source: Pollitz *et al.* (2001).

Albany, New York – a market whose regulatory rules, insurance products, and prices were then (and are now) very similar to those in New Jersey. In Albany, all applicants consistently received clean offers of coverage and all were quoted the same community rate. On average, single applicants were quoted premiums of $342 per month – much higher than the lowest rate quoted for similar coverage in the underwritten markets studied ($34 per month), but also much lower than the highest rate ($2,504).

Other state approaches to regulating underwriting practices

New Jersey is not alone in its comprehensive approach to regulating individual health insurance. Four other states (Table 8.2) – New York, Vermont, Massachusetts, and Maine – have similar rules, although Massachusetts and Maine do permit limited premium adjustments on the basis of age. Residents of these states, regardless of their health status, are also are guaranteed the right to buy individual health insurance that will cover a guaranteed package of benefits. All coverage is available for a community rate that, while not inexpensive, is predictable.

Everywhere else in the United States, consumers have fewer protections when buying individual health insurance. The approaches of other states can be categorized into roughly four groups. (See Table 8.2.)

The second two regulatory approaches – "portability" and "carrier of last resort" – provide for guaranteed issue protections for at least some residents, at least some of the time. "Portability" states (thirteen) offer a subset of qualified residents – usually those with prior continuous group coverage – some protection from medical underwriting. Qualified residents can buy an individual policy on a guaranteed issue basis when they first leave employer-based coverage. Most states in this group also set minimum standards for the benefits portability plans must cover, though

Table 8.2 State approaches to individual insurance market regulation

Comprehensive (5)	*Portability (13)*	*Carrier of last resort (6)*	*High-risk pool only (22)*	*Minimalist (5)*
ME[a] MA[a] NJ[a] NY[a] VT[a]	CA[a] FL[b] GA[a] ID[a] IA[a] MN[a] MT[a] NV[a] OH[a] OR[a] RI SD[a] WA[a]	DC HI[a] MI[a] NC PA[a] VA	AK AR CO CT IL IN KS KY LA MD MS MO NE NH NM ND[a] OK SC TX UT WI WY	AL AZ DE TN WV

Source: www.healthinsuranceinfo.net

Notes

a Some rating reforms apply.

b Rating reforms apply to only certain residents eligible for portability protections.

Regulations in place as of April, 2003.

few require standardized benefits as comprehensive as those in New Jersey. As a result, coverage limits typically found in individual health plans may also exist in portability plans. Further, in all but one of these states (Rhode Island), rating rules protect qualified residents by limiting the degree to which premiums can vary, if at all, based on health status.[2]

Portability protections are designed to help one substantial portion of consumers who need individual coverage – those who lose access to group coverage, for example, when they lose their job, retire, or lose dependent status under their parents' plan. However, unless expanded or combined with other safeguards, portability protections leave out other residents – those who have to move from one individual health plan to another, or those who experience a break in coverage as short as one month. For this reason, several portability states (Iowa, Nevada, and South Dakota) have adopted additional rules enabling people to switch from one individual health plan to another without medical underwriting, at least under certain circumstances. In addition, six portability states (California, Iowa, Minnesota, Montana, Oregon, and Washington) also operate high-risk pools to offer safety net coverage for residents who don't qualify for portability protections.[3]

"Carrier of last resort" states (six) designate at least one carrier – usually Blue Cross Blue Shield – to offer individual policies to all residents, regardless of health status. In three of these states (Hawaii, Michigan, and Pennsylvania), the carrier of last resort must also use community rating. Years ago this model was the most prevalent approach to protecting access to individual health insurance coverage. Most states have since abandoned it, concerned the carrier of last resort could not survive financially in underwritten markets. However, some carriers appear to not only survive but thrive. In 2002, Pennsylvania's Blue Cross Blue Shield plans, which sell guaranteed issue and community-rated coverage while the competition medically underwrites, were found to have surplus reserves of $3 billion, far in excess of state solvency requirements (Ditzen 2002).

"High-risk pool only" states (the twenty-two states listed in Table 8.2) generally do not limit medical underwriting in the individual health insurance market. All residents, regardless of coverage history, can be turned down or charged more because of their health status. High-risk pools offer safety net coverage to people whom private insurers turn away. By definition high-risk pools incur heavy losses that must be publicly subsidized. To limit the need to raise taxes, states often try to minimize pool losses by setting high premiums or imposing high cost sharing or other coverage limits. As a result very few people tend to take advantage of high-risk pool coverage. The combined enrollment in these twenty-two state high-risk pools is less than 100,000 people (Achman and Chollett 2001).

The remaining "minimalist protection" states (five) also permit medical underwriting in individual health insurance, but offer no safety net for their uninsurable residents. People have only the protections guaranteed under the 1996 Health Insurance Portability and Accountability Act (HIPAA) – guaranteed issue coverage from private insurers with no other rating or benefit protections.[4]

Other state strategies

These five broad categories only begin to distinguish between the regulatory approaches different states have employed. For example, Washington has adopted a unique framework for its portability strategy. Qualified applicants for individual coverage cannot be medically underwritten. For all others, however, the underwriting process poses no uncertainty because all insurers must use a common published health screen.[5] Each health condition is assigned a point value. For example, the score for metastatic breast cancer is 1,200, compared to 70 for hypertension with no other complications. Non-portability residents with a score of 330 or higher can be turned down by insurers and are eligible to seek coverage from the high-risk pool. Those with a score below 330, however, must be offered guaranteed issue, community-rated coverage by private carriers.[6] The standardized health screen not only simplifies the insurance application process for consumers, it gives the state a tool for controlling the amount of risk carriers cede to the publicly subsidized high-risk pool.

Other states look beyond the individual market to the group insurance market to guarantee access to coverage and spread risk. New Mexico, for example, allows HIPAA-eligible individuals and certain self-employed sole proprietors to buy small-group coverage from the state's small-employer purchasing pool. (Federal law requires all small-group policies to be sold on a guaranteed issue basis.) Eleven other states permit self-employed groups of one to buy small-group policies.[7]

Eight states have comprehensive group conversion laws that regulate both the content and the cost of conversion policies.[8] Consumers leaving group health plans may convert their group coverage to a non-group policy, though their claims experience remains at least partially pooled with the carrier's other group business.

Finally, thirty-nine states have adopted state continuation laws, similar to COBRA, that allow former small-group health plan participants to continue coverage temporarily under the group insurance policy.[9] People who elect this option also continue to have their claims experience pooled with other group market participants.

These various group market-based strategies may act as a safety valve, diverting some high-risk applicants who might otherwise need individual coverage back into the larger and more stable group market.

Politics of market reform

A thorough comparative analysis of these different state regulatory approaches has never been conducted. Such a study would certainly inform public debate over the advisability of limiting risk selection by insurers in health insurance markets. Instead, the current debate is largely political and highly charged. Pros and cons of market reform are seldom discussed objectively and accurately. For example, the Coalition Against Guaranteed Issue publicly denounces market reforms in the strongest possible terms. Guaranteed issue "causes insane pricing for health insurance" and "ruins the market for everyone," according to the Coalition's website, which also invites visitors to "find out why it costs less to lease [a] Ferrari than get a $500-deductible healthcare policy in New Jersey."[10] Another group, the US Freedom Foundation, seeks to circumvent state guaranteed issue and community rating laws by permitting the establishment of Internet Health Insurance Plans, which would be governed only by the laws of the insurer's home state even when purchased on-line by consumers in other states. According to this group's news release, "consumers in states with outrageous premium rates such as New Jersey, Massachusetts, Vermont, and Maine would have immediate relief, finding policies for up to two-thirds less than premium prices in their home state."[11]

Nowhere in the hyperbole of these messages are the real tradeoffs of market reform revealed. Repeal of New Jersey's individual market regulation would allow the sale of lower-cost policies – probably covering fewer benefits – to young adults in good health. However, older and less healthy residents who are insured today would likely see premiums skyrocket and possibly lose their individual coverage. Would repeal result in a net increase in the number of New Jersey residents with insurance? Perhaps not. Most uninsured have very low incomes, below 200 percent of poverty, and would be hard pressed to afford even $100 per month for insurance. Age-rated underwritten policies are available in other states for far less, but they offer far less coverage with very high annual deductibles ($1,000 to $5,000) and other cost sharing. Research shows such bare bones policies are unlikely to benefit the low-income uninsured and are unpopular with consumers (Glied *et al.* 2002).

Even if repeal of comprehensive market reform such as New Jersey's would produce a net increase in the number of insured residents, state policymakers would need to consider other issues. For example, what would happen to older and sicker consumers who lose coverage? It has been well documented that the sick uninsured receive less care, later care, and poorer-quality care compared to the sick insured.[12] Moreover, a number of studies demonstrate that loss of health insurance benefits can have adverse consequences for health status (see Levy and Meltzer 2001). Consequently disenfranchising today's market participants might well negatively impact public health and uncompensated care. In New Jersey's case, the state might avert these problems by offering safety net coverage through a high-risk pool. However, the number of individual market participants in New Jersey today is roughly comparable to the combined enrollment of all state high-risk pools in the United States in 2001. Collectively, in that year these programs incurred over $400 million in net losses that had to be publicly subsidized (Communicating for Agriculture 2002). Policymakers would need to weigh such costs in the context of the state's current fiscal crisis.

In the end, the politics and policy of individual market regulation remain a challenge. Access to affordable individual health insurance will be difficult to sustain in regulated and unregulated markets alike. The different approaches to spreading risk only shift costs around and the trade-offs are difficult. By contrast, external subsidies could make coverage more affordable, but the political and fiscal capacity to fund subsidies is limited. Caught in this bind, state policymakers will need to decide which second-best solution can be sustained in the near term. And hope for better times.

Notes

1 New Jersey Department of Banking and Insurance, Individual Health Coverage Program Rates, June 2003, http://www.state.nj.us/dobi/singplnh.htm. Downloaded July 10, 2003.

2 Florida's portability reforms offer rating protections to only some residents with prior continuous coverage – those most recently covered under state-regulated group health insurance policies. Floridians whose prior coverage was under a self-insured group health plan have no rating protections in the individual insurance market.

3 Florida is a seventh portability state in this category with a high-risk pool. However, Florida's pool has been closed to new enrollment for over a decade.

4 Alabama is included in this category even though its approach is somewhat different from the other four states. In Alabama, people who are HIPAA-eligible can buy coverage from the state high-risk pool. This program is not available to other uninsurable residents, however. In this respect, Alabama offers market

protections only to HIPAA-eligible residents with no other safety net access for the uninsurable.

5 See http://www.insurance.wa.gov/consumers/rates/individualmain.asp.

6 Washington regulators originally set the threshold underwriting score of 330 to assure that the most expensive 8 percent of individual market participants would be covered under the high-risk pool. Based on revised estimates, the threshold was lowered in 2003 in order to yield the target high-risk pool enrollment. See Song (2003).

7 These states are Colorado, Connecticut, Delaware, Florida, Maine, Maryland, Massachusetts, New Hampshire, North Carolina, Vermont, and Washington.

8 These states are Florida, Georgia, Idaho, Minnesota, Montana, Nevada, Ohio, and Utah.

9 States that do not have such continuation laws are Alabama, Alaska, Arizona, Delaware, Hawaii, Idaho, Indiana, Michigan, Montana, Pennsylvania, and Virginia. In Washington, insurers are required to offer small employers the option of continuation coverage, but small-group contracts are not mandated to include this benefit.

10 See www.cagionline.org.

11 News release, March 11, 2003, available at www.freedomfoundation.us/news_releases.

12 See, for example, Institute of Medicine (2002) and Hadley (2003).

References

Achman, L. and Chollet, D. (2001) "Insuring the Uninsurable: An Overview of State High-risk Pools." Commonwealth Fund.

Communicating for Agriculture (2002) "Comprehensive Health Insurance for High-risk Individuals." Fergus Falls, MN.

Ditzen, L.S. (2002) "Cash-rich Insurers sit on Billion in Surplus." *Philadelphia Inquirer*, February 24, p. A01.

Glied, S., Callahan, C., Mays, J., and Edwards, J. (2002) "Bare-bones Health Plans: Are they Worth the Money?" Report for the Commonwealth Fund.

Hadley, J. (2003) "Sick and Poorer: The Consequences of being Uninsured." *Medical Care Research and Review*, 60 (2): 35–75.

Institute of Medicine (2002) "Care without Coverage: Too Little, Too Late." Washington DC: National Academy Press.

Levitt, K., Smith, C., Cowan, C., Lazenby, H., Sensenig, A., and Catlin, A. (2003) "Trends in US Health Care Spending, 2001." *Health Affairs*, 22 (1): 154–164.

Levy, H. and Meltzer, D. (2001) "What do we Really Know about whether Health Insurance Affects Health?" Economic Research Initiative on the Uninsured Working Paper 6, Ann Arbor, MI: University of Michigan and Robert Wood Johnson Foundation, December 20. Available at www.umich.edu/~eriu/pdf/wp6.pdf. Accessed September 10, 2003.

Pollitz, K., Sorian, R., and Thomas, K. (2001) "How Accessible is Individual Health Insurance for Consumers in Less than Perfect Health?" Menlo Park, CA: Kaiser Family Foundation.

Song, K.M. (2003) "More of the Sickest People Must Enter Costlier Pool." *Seattle Times*, June 26.

Part IV

Reforming insurance market reform

What are the possibilities? What are the alternatives?

9 How can reform work better?

M. Susan Marquis

In voluntary, unregulated insurance markets, health insurers will try to separate consumers into distinct risk groups and set premiums to cover the expected costs of care for each group. As a result, however, the highest-risk individuals may be unable to find affordable insurance or may be denied insurance. Insurance regulations are aimed at helping the sick obtain coverage by limiting insurers' ability to segment risk and forcing more risk pooling. However, if insurers are unable to segment risk, adverse selection – a greater likelihood of participation in the market by higher-risk consumers than by lower-risk consumers – may occur. For the market as a whole, adverse selection may drive prices to a level at which the market is not viable or at least not attractive to low risks. Individual insurers who experience adverse selection will suffer losses and will be unwilling to supply insurance. Insurers thus have an incentive to adopt new means to segment the market to avoid adverse selection. If they are able to do so, then regulations may not help in making insurance available and affordable for the sick.

In this chapter, I consider policy options that might enhance the effectiveness of reforms by overcoming fears of adverse selection. These options include:

- Risk adjustment: prospective adjustment and retrospective risk sharing.
- High-risk pools.
- Purchasing cooperatives.

In evaluating these options, I will address their effectiveness in overcoming insurers' concerns about adverse selection and whether they are likely to broaden risk pools and expand coverage.

Is adverse selection real?

Before turning to these policy options, however, let us briefly look at the extent of adverse selection with market regulation. The evidence on this point is mixed and inconclusive. Most quantitative studies suggest that small-group and individual market reforms have not led to serious adverse selection in the market as a whole. A study of New Jersey's individual insurance market reforms found no evidence of adverse selection (Swartz and Garnick 1999) although more recent data suggest that the market has experienced steep enrollment declines, rising premiums, and retention of poorer health risks (Monheit *et al.* 2004). Additionally, a study of New York's individual and small-group reforms suggested that the risk profile of those purchasing insurance was not altered by reforms, though more recent data suggest that the individual insurance market in New York has become unattractive to low risks (Coughlin and Lutzky 2002). A few studies have reported that market regulations were associated with a modest increase in coverage for higher-risk individuals (measured by age or expected health expenditures) or small-employer groups (measured by industry) at the expense of lower-risk individual or groups (Sloan and Conover 1998, Hing and Jensen 1999; Simon 2000; Monheit and Schone 2004). On the other hand, qualitative evidence suggests that comprehensive regulations in the individual market led to more substantial adverse selection in the individual insurance market in some states – and produced marked instability in two states – Kentucky and Washington (Hall 2000; Kirk 2000; Fox, Cantor, Cuite 2002).

Furthermore, restrictions on underwriting and pricing only enhance insurers' incentives to find other ways to avoid enrolling the sick and attracting only the healthy patients, who are expected to be profitable ("cream skimming"). Insurers may design plans to attract only the good risks, for example, by structuring the cost-sharing requirements, by offering benefits that are attractive to healthier patients such as preventive care, or by excluding benefits that are attractive to higher-risk patients (Van de Ven and Ellis 2000; Newhouse 1994). They also might select by the design of their provider panel, for example, excluding physicians with the best reputation for treating certain high-cost conditions or by strict utilization management and limited specialty referrals (Van de Ven and Ellis 2000; Newhouse 1994). They may give poor service to the ill to encourage them to go elsewhere (Van Barneveld *et al.* 1996). They may also use marketing practices to try to attract healthier patients (Maibach *et al.* 1998). There is some evidence to suggest that insurers do respond to market regulation by finding new ways to segment the market (Kirk 2000; Feldvebel and Sky 2000; Berry and White 2000). What are the mechanisms to overcome these responses to regulation?

Risk adjustment

Insurers have an incentive to select healthier patients when they are unable to vary premiums based on risk (Pauly 1984). Risk adjustment is intended to eliminate or at least reduce these incentives by redistributing premiums so that payments to a plan match the expected cost for the enrollee. It deals with the supply price of insurance – the payment to the plan for its enrollees. The supply price relative to expected costs will affect plans' incentives to screen out the sick in some fashion. If they are the same, plans have no incentive to cream-skim.

Prospective risk adjustment

Prospective risk adjustment sets payments at the start of the period based on demographic and diagnostic information available at that time. Conceptually, prospective risk adjustment is preferable to adjustment models that use information that becomes known during the period (retrospective adjustment), because the goal is to adjust for expected risk or the risk that can be known by the insurer, and not for bad luck or the random variations in health care spending that occur over the period (Newhouse *et al.* 1997).

How well risk adjustment will overcome insurers' incentives to select healthy risks depends upon how well the factors used in assessing risk explain variations in expected costs. There has been extensive research on possible risk adjusters. However, most of these fall far short of explaining the 20–25 percent of the variation in actual costs that is generally considered knowable (Newhouse 1996; Van de Ven and Ellis 2000). Although risk adjustment may not need to be perfect to eliminate insurers' expected profit from selecting healthy risks and thereby eliminate the incentive to do so, Newhouse (1996) suggests that insurers only need to be able to predict a few percentage points more than the adjusters to reap substantial profits from adopting behaviors to select favorable risks. The conclusion then is that existing prospective risk adjustment technology is unlikely to solve the problem.

Whether current risk adjustment technology overcomes selection problems is an empirical question that has only indirectly been answered. Risk adjustment in the private sector is practically nonexistent, which may indicate that the costs of doing so outweigh the gains. A 2001 conference concluded that private employers do not use risk adjustment to deal with selection problems because they have alternative strategies that are effective and less costly (Glazer and McGuire 2001).

Risk adjustment requires extensive data collection effort – in some cases more than insurers currently undertake in underwriting (Keenan *et al.* 2001). While risk adjustment is intended to make plans neutral in selecting patients, the method has been criticized as creating inappropriate incentives for plans to invest in health-improving activities and to distort information that is part of the adjustment formula (Van de Ven and Ellis 2000). The latter is analogous to DRG creep that was found in response to the Medicare Prospective Payment System.

Retrospective risk sharing

Under retrospective risk sharing, plans are reimbursed *ex post* for some of their costs of enrolling higher-cost cases. This will reduce incentives for cream skimming, but the concern is that reimbursement based on incurred costs will reduce incentives to hold down costs. Risk sharing may take one of several forms.

Threshold reinsurance

Plans may be reimbursed some share of the actual costs for any member whose expenditures exceed some threshold. For example, under New York's Healthy New York Program the state acts as reinsurer for enrollees in the program with expenditures above $30,000 – it pays up to 90 percent of the costs of their claims between $30,000 and $100,000 (Swartz and Keenan 2001). New Jersey's "pay or play" requirement included in the individual market reforms of 1992 provided reinsurance for carriers issuing individual coverage. Kathy Swartz has offered several alternative reinsurance proposals for strengthening the individual insurance market (Swartz 2001, 2002).

Reinsurance would reduce the consequences of enrolling bad risks and so decrease incentives for selection. However, plans may still benefit from spending resources on attracting good risks. Moreover, it also reimburses plans for bad luck, which is not necessary to eliminate selection issues. Reinsurance may also decrease incentives to efficiently manage costs because the plan may not bear the cost consequences of doing so. This can be improved by varying the level of insurer liability over different ranges of expenditure and so require that insurers bear some cost of inefficiency (Swartz 2002).

Proportional risk sharing

Joe Newhouse has argued for reimbursing plans prospectively for a share of the costs of any member (Newhouse 1994; Newhouse *et al.* 1997). This strategy, in effect, uses actual use as a risk adjuster, and is referred to as "partial capitation." He argues that any risk adjustment scheme that uses diagnoses incorporates implicit judgments about appropriate treatment patterns, but this could lead to underprovision of discretionary services. Incorporating use as a risk adjuster protects against underprovision of services or "stinting" on quality. On the other hand, it also reduces the cost of overprovision of service. In contrast to threshold reinsurance, proportional risk adjustment reduces the benefits from enrolling the healthiest cases, and so may have a stronger effect on selection incentives than threshold reinsurance.

Risk sharing for high-risk cases

A different reinsurance type of proposal, offered in the Dutch context, would have each insurer designate, ex ante, a certain percentage of its members whose costs would be covered by a common pool (Van Barneveld *et al.* 1996). This proposal differs from a high-risk pool, which will be discussed later, in that the high-risk persons have the same benefits and pay the same premiums as others in the plan. The high-risk persons themselves need not be aware of the risk-sharing arrangement. In this approach, insurers are not reimbursed for the unpredictable spending by better risks, as occurs with other reinsurance schemes. However, plans that have no high-risk members receive some compensation for the riskiest of their patients, while plans with a flood of high-risk members receive compensation only for the designated share. Moreover, such an approach may not be useful for new applicants because plans only have information about expected use over time (Newhouse *et al.* 1997).

Condition-specific risk sharing

Some have suggested reimbursing plans for patients with specified high-cost illness to diminish plans' incentives to select healthy patients (Luft 1986). If the amount of the payment is prospectively set, even though the disease occurrence is retrospectively determined, incentives for efficiency are preserved. (Though concerns about underservice may arise.) The New York 1996 insurance reform law established a medical conditions risk pool, but insurers were reimbursed a portion of the actual costs incurred in covering the specified conditions (Hall 2000); that is, the payment was also retrospectively determined. Implementation of a condition-specific risk pool is likely to engender political battles over which conditions should and should not be included in the pool, may impinge on patient privacy, and is subject to diagnosis inflation (Swartz 1995).

Risk adjustment and incentives for preferred risk selection

While there is limited experience with risk adjustments, simulation analyses have demonstrated that they have the potential to substantially limit problems of adverse selection. A simulation of alternative risk-sharing approaches in the Dutch context suggested that high-risk risk sharing for the top 4 percent of risks would reduce the predictable losses for bad risks by about 50 percent, a substantial change in the incentive to select (Van Barneveld *et al.* 1996). For the same reinsurer payment, the reduction in predictable losses for bad risks was about 40 percent under threshold risk sharing and 20 percent with proportional risk sharing (Van Barneveld *et al.* 1998). The relative performance of different strategies, however, would depend on choices about the fraction of enrollees included, the threshold for risk sharing, and the proportion of risk shared. Keeler *et al.* (1998) conducted some simulations that suggested that proportional and threshold risk sharing each reduced losses of a plan experiencing adverse selection by about 50 percent, and condition-specific risk sharing decreased it about 66 percent. Another simulation comparing different approaches concluded that risk sharing for high risks was superior to either proportional risk sharing or threshold reinsurance in limiting incentives for cream skimming and preserving incentives for efficiency (Van Barneveld *et al.* 2001).

Risk adjustment and coverage expansions

As noted above, risk adjustment alters the supply price of insurance – the amount that the insurer receives for each enrollee. Coverage rates, however, will depend on the demand price of insurance – the amount that each enrollee must pay to purchase coverage. The supply price and demand price need not be the same (Van de Ven and Ellis 2000). For example, the amount paid to a plan on behalf of a particular enrollee may differ from the amount the enrollee pays for the coverage because of risk-adjustment payments to the plan or because the enrollee payment is subsidized. Thus, the effects of risk adjustment on coverage rates will depend importantly on other decisions about the implementation of the risk-adjustment strategy that affect the demand price – especially whether the risk adjustment is financed internally or externally.

If premiums are community-rated and risk adjustment involves an internal redistribution of premiums collected in a given market, say the individual market, then risk adjustment may have little effect on overall coverage rates. Community rating will still result in higher prices for the healthy and lower prices for the sick than would occur when insurers can segment risks. The cost of high-risk persons will be borne by low-risk purchasers who remain in the market and the high premiums for low-risk purchasers may drive them from the market. This can be mitigated somewhat by risk-adjusting premium payments as well to allow some variation between rates paid by those of different health status. For example, consumer payments may also be allowed to vary within limits by age or other factors.

However, coverage expansions are likely to require subsidies that would spread the risk of high-cost cases more broadly than among the low-risk people in the market in question and lower the demand price. Direct subsidies to individuals' premium payments through tax deductions are one example. External financing of some of the risk-adjustment payments is another approach. A state-financed reinsurance program, as in New York's Healthy New York program, is another example (Swartz 2001). Paying for high-cost claims through general taxes spreads these costs more broadly to all taxpayers and not just the healthy that remain in the market in question. This would keep premiums down and may attract more new healthy participants to the market as well as the less healthy, further helping to lower premiums. Lowering premiums to attract participants was a primary objective of the Healthy New York reinsurance scheme (Swartz and Keenan 2001). However, much research suggests that subsidies will need to be quite large to lower premiums sufficiently to induce many low-income uninsured to buy coverage (Long and Marquis 2002; Marquis and Long 1995).

High-risk pools

State high-risk pools for individuals who are unable to obtain insurance have been in existence since Connecticut and Minnesota introduced the first pools in 1976 (Bovbjerg and Koller, 1986). Currently thirty states operate high-risk pools to offer coverage to those who are unable to obtain coverage in the individual insurance market (Chollet 2002). High-risk pools are similar to the concept of risk sharing for high risks as noted above, except that the high-risk cases are covered in a separate insurance plan and have benefits and premiums that may differ from the market as a whole. For example, Washington state's Health Insurance Reform Act of 2000 allows health insurers to screen out 8 percent of applicants for individual insurance who are considered high risk, with the expectation that these individuals can enroll in the state's high-risk pool.

The ability to refer high-risk cases to a high-risk pool should limit insurer incentives to compete on the basis of risk selection. Premiums in the risk pool are also usually partially subsidized. They are typically capped at a fixed percentage (usually about 150) of rates charged by private insurers for standard risks. Where tight rating regulations prevail, risk pools may also help coverage among lower-risk persons by spreading the burden of higher-risk persons beyond purchasers in the specific market if some of the costs of the risk pool are financed through general taxes or by premium assessments across the entire market.

The subsidy should promote demand among higher-risk individuals. However, evidence suggests that most of these pools cover only a small share of the target population. Best estimates are that the pools reach only 5–25 percent of the target population (based on US GAO 1996; Laudicina 1988; Stearns *et al.* 1997). High premiums in many pools, despite the subsidy, appear to be a barrier to participation (Stearns and Mroz 1995), and analysis of disenrollments from risk plans also shows that price is a factor in participation (Stearns and Mroz 1995). Thus, unless states subsidize risk pools more heavily than in the past or attract a broader risk pool to lower premiums, it is unlikely that they are a solution to the problem of the uninsured.

Purchasing cooperatives

Purchasing cooperatives are a concept that many would encourage to help markets operate more effectively. Purchasing cooperatives involve collective purchasing by businesses or individuals or both. The cooperative contracts with health plans on behalf of cooperative members and performs a number of administrative functions such as selling and billing. By consolidating administrative functions, some argue that purchasing cooperatives can help lower the price by realizing economies of scale in administration. By grouping small businesses or individuals into a collective purchasing unit, the cooperatives may also enhance purchasing power and be able to strike better deals with insurers than the individual members would be able to negotiate operating independently. Some also believe that cooperatives can be an effective vehicle for greater risk pooling.

To date, most cooperatives have failed to gain a price advantage for pool participants and so have not reduced the number of uninsured (Long and Marquis 2001; Wicks 2002). Lack of sufficient scale is often cited as a key factor preventing the cooperatives from gaining administrative efficiencies or purchasing power that could lead to lower prices (Long and Marquis 2001; Wicks 2002). A number of proposals for reducing the uninsured that have included cooperatives as one component of the strategy have therefore included mandates for purchasing through the cooperative or incentives to do so (for example, Gruber 2001; Singer *et al.* 2001). Nonetheless, it seems unlikely that cooperatives alone are likely to reduce prices sufficiently to attract large numbers of the uninsured to opt for coverage.

Moreover, experience suggests that voluntary purchasing cooperatives are not able to pool risk beyond the practices in the market outside of the cooperative. Should the cooperative try to do so, the cooperative itself will experience adverse selection and ultimately fail or inadvertently become just a high-risk pool (Wicks 2002). For example, if the cooperative practices community rating, but the rest of the market does not, then healthy groups are likely to find prices in the cooperative to be higher than prices they would pay outside of the cooperative; as a result they will not participate in the cooperative. In contrast, high-risk groups are likely to find the cooperative to be attractive, at least in the short run. A corollary of this problem is adverse selection across markets that are subject to different regulatory rules – for example, the exemption of association plans from reforms in Kentucky is credited by some observers as an important factor destabilizing the market (Hall 2002; Feldvebel and Sky 2000). In addition, adverse selection between cooperatives may be an issue if competing cooperatives are permitted in a service area. Addressing risk selection is thus an important design consideration in setting up purchasing cooperatives.

However, purchasing cooperatives may carry out a number of administrative functions that may help markets work more effectively. Cooperatives could carry out risk adjustment for health plans selling to cooperative members. Cooperatives can require a minimum level of coverage and some standardization of benefits, which would reduce insurer's ability to use plan design to select the most preferred risks. However, this may also reduce the ability of the market to respond to consumer preferences. Purchasing cooperatives can also set rules for plans wishing to sell through the cooperative regarding service areas, marketing practices, and physician contracting that would cut off some other avenues for preferred risk selection on the part of plans. Cooperatives may also gather, synthesize, and disseminate information about plan performance and quality that can help in limiting plan's ability to use service or treatment patterns as a means of selecting preferred risk.

Conclusions

Insurance market reforms are intended to increase access to coverage for high-risk individuals. Prospective risk adjustment, reinsurance schemes, or high-risk pools are all strategies that may help to overcome insurers' concerns about adverse selection, thus limiting incentives for favorable risk selection and helping to stabilize the market. In this way, market reforms may improve access for high-risk individuals. Despite such efforts to improve reform implementation, significant gains in the number of insured are likely to require substantial subsidies to lower the price that consumers pay for coverage. Policy solutions to cover the uninsured, to protect both high- and low-risk people, and to maintain a stable insurance market are likely to require a mix of strategies.

References

Berry, J. and White, R. (2000) "An Insurer's Perspective on Reform." *Journal of Health Politics, Policy and Law*, 25 (1): 205–210.

Bovbjerg, R. and Koller, C. (1986) "State Health Insurance Pools: Current Performance, Future Prospects." *Inquiry*, 23 (2): 111–121.

Chollet, D. (2002) "Expanding Individual Health Insurance Coverage: Are High-risk Pools the Answer?" *Health Affairs* (Web Exclusives), 23 October: W349–352.

Coughlin, T.A. and. Lutzky, A.W. (2002) "Recent Changes in Health Policy for Low-income People in New York." *Assessing the New Federalism*, State Update No. 22, Washington, DC: Urban Institute.

Cutler, D.M. and Zeckhauser, R.J. (1997) "Adverse Selection in Health Insurance." Working paper 6107, Cambridge, MA: National Bureau of Economic Research.

Cutler, D.M. and Zeckhauser, R.J. (2002) "The Anatomy of Health Insurance" in A.J. Culyer and J.P. Newhouse (eds), *Handbook of Health Insurance*, 1A, Amsterdam: Elsevier Press.

Feldvebel, A.K. and Sky, D. (2000) "A Regulator's Perspective on Other States' Experiences." *Journal of Health Politics, Policy, and Law*, 25 (1): 197–204.

Fox, K., Cantor, J.C., and Cuite, C. (2002) *Market and Regulatory Reforms to Expand Health Insurance Coverage*. Report 4.1.5, Washington State Planning Grant on Access to Health Insurance, submitted to Office of Financial Management, Office of the Governor of Washington State, April.

Glazer, J. and McGuire, T.G. (2001) "Why Don't Private Employers Use Risk Adjustment?" Conference Overview, *Inquiry*, 38 (3): 242–244.

Gruber, J. (2001) "A Private/Public Partnership for National Health Insurance" in J.A. Meyer and E.K. Wicks (eds), *Covering America*, Washington, DC: Economic and Social Research Institute.

Hall, M.A. (2000) "An Evaluation of New York's Reform Law." *Journal of Health Politics, Policy, and Law*, 25 (1): 71–99.

Hall, M.A. (2002) "Of Magic Wands and Kaleidoscopes: Fixing Problems in the Individual Market." *Health Affairs* (Web Exclusives), 23 October: W353–358.

Hing, E. and Jensen, G. (1999) "Health Insurance Portability and Accountability Act of 1996: Lesson from the States." *Medical Care*, 37 (7): 692–705.

Keeler, E.B., Carter, G., and Newhouse, J.P. (1998) "A Model of the Impact of Reimbursement Schemes on Health Plan Choice." *Journal of Health Economics*, 17 (3): 297–320.

Keenan, P.S., Buntin, M.J.B., McGuire, T.G., and Newhouse, J.P. (2001) "The Prevalence of Formal Risk Adjustment in Health Plan Purchasing." *Inquiry*, 38 (3): 245–257.

Kirk, A. (2000) "Riding the Bull: Experience with Individual Market Reform in Washington, Kentucky, and Massachusetts." *Journal of Health Politics, Policy, and Law*, 25 (1): 133–173.

Laudicina, S. (1988) "State Health Risk Pools: Insuring the 'Uninsurable'." *Health Affairs*, 7 (4): 97–104.

Long, S.H. and Marquis, M.S. (2001) "Have Small Group Health Insurance Purchasing Alliances Increased Coverage?" *Health Affairs*, 20: 154–167.

Long, S.H. and Marquis, M.S. (2002) "Participation in a Public Insurance Program: Subsidies, Crowd-out and Adverse Selection." *Inquiry*, 39 (3): 243–257.

Luft, H.S. (1986) "Compensating for Biased Selection in Health Insurance." *Milbank Quarterly*, 64: 566–591.

Maibach, E., Dusenberry, K., Zupp, P. *et al.* (1998) "Marketing HMOs to Medicare Beneficiaries: An Analysis of Four Medicare Markets." Menlo Park, CA: Kaiser Family Foundation.

Marquis, M.S. and Long, S.H. (1995) "Worker Demand for Health Insurance in the Non-group Market." *Journal of Health Economics*, 14 (1): 47–63.

Monheit, A.C. and Schone, B. (2004) "How has Small Group Market Reform Affected Employee Health Insurance Coverage?" *Journal of Public Economics*, 88 (1–2): 237–254.

Monheit, A.C., Cantor, J.C., Koller, M., and Fox, K.S. (2004) "Community Rating and Sustainable Health Insurance Markets in New Jersey." *Health Affairs* 23 (4). In press.

Newhouse, J.P. (1994) "Patients at Risk; Health Reform and Risk Adjustment." *Health Affairs*, 13: 132–146.

Newhouse, J.P. (1996) "Reimbursing Health Plans and Health Providers: Efficiency in Production versus Selection." *Journal of Economic Literature*, 34: 1236–1263.

Newhouse, J.P., Buntin, M.B., and Chapman, J.D. (1997) "Risk Adjustment and Medicare: Taking a Closer Look." *Health Affairs*, 16 (5): 26–43.

Pauly, M.V. (1984) "Is Cream-skimming a Problem for the Competitive Medical Market?" *Journal of Health Economics*, 3 (1): 87–96.

Simon, K. (2000) "The Effect of State Insurance Regulation on Price and Availability of Health Benefits in Small Firms: Econometrics and Economic Theory." Working paper 2001, East Lansing, MI: Department of Economics, Michigan State University.

Singer, S.J., Garber, A.M., and Enthoven, A.C. (2001) "Near-universal Coverage through Health Plan Competition" in J.A. Meyer and E.K. Wicks (eds), *Covering America*, Washington, DC: Economic and Social Research Institute.

Sloan, F.A. and Conover, C.J. (1998) "Effects of State Reforms on Health Insurance Coverage of Adults." *Inquiry*, 35 (3): 280–292.

Stearns, S.C. and Mroz, T.A. (1995) "Premium Increases and Disenrollment from State Risk Pools," *Inquiry*, 32: 392–406.

Stearns, S.C., Slifkin, R.T., Thorpe, K.E., and Mroz, T.A. (1997) "The Structure and Experience of State Risk Pools, 1988–1994." *Medical Care Research and Review*, 54: 224–238.

Swartz, K. (1995) "Reducing Risk Selection Requires more than Risk Adjustments." *Inquiry*, 32 (1): 6–13.

Swartz, K. (2001) "Markets for Individual Health Insurance: Can we Make them Work with Incentives to Purchase Insurance?" *Inquiry*, 38 (2): 133–145.

Swartz, K. (2002) "Government as Reinsure for Very-high-cost Persons in Non-group Health Insurance Markets." *Health Affairs* (Web Exclusives), 23 October: W380–382.

Swartz, K. and Garnick, D. (1999) "Can Adverse Selection be avoided in a Market for Individual Health Insurance?" *Medical Care Research and Review*, 56 (3): 373–388.

Swartz, K. and Keenan, P.S. (2001) "Healthy New York: Making Insurance More Affordable for Low-income Workers." Report 484, New York: Commonwealth Fund.

USGAO, US General Accounting Office (1996) *Private Health Insurance: Millions relying on Individual Market face Cost and Coverage Trade-offs*. GAO/HEHS-97–8, Washington, DC: USGAO.

Van Barneveld, E.M., van Vliet, R.C.J.A., and van de Ven, W.P.M.M. (1996) "Mandatory High-risk Pooling: An Approach to Reducing Incentives for Cream Skimming." *Inquiry*, 33 (2): 133–154.

Van Barneveld, E.M., van Vliet, R.C.J.A., and van de Ven, W.R.M.M. (1998) "Mandatory Pooling as a Supplement to Risk Adjusted Capitation Payments in a Competitive Health Insurance Market." *Social Science and Medicine*, 47: 223–232.

Van Barneveld, E.M., Lamers, L.M., van Vliet, R.C.J.A., and van de Ven, W.R.M.M. (2001) "Risk Sharing as a Supplement to Imperfect Capitation: a Tradeoff between Selection and Efficiency." *Journal of Health Economics*, 20 (2): 147–168.

Van de Ven, W.P.M.M. and Ellis, R.P. (2000) "Risk Adjustment in Competitive Health Plan Markets" in A.J. Culyer and J.P. Newhouse (eds), *Handbook of Health Insurance*, 1A, Amsterdam: Elsevier Press.

Wicks, E.K. (2002) "Health Insurance Purchasing Cooperatives, Task Force on the Future of Health Insurance." New York: Commonwealth Fund.

10 Improving state insurance market reform

What's left to try?

Len M. Nichols

Insurance market reform laws and regulations were passed in response to the small-business community's virtually universal plea for relief from repeated double-digit premium increases and insurers' refusals to renew disruptions in the small-group market (USGAO 1992). Insurance market regulatory power had rested with the states for some time (Nichols and Blumberg 1998), but the premium inflation of the late 1980s and early 1990s pushed many local systems to crisis point, and, along with the recession of 1991–1992, arguably contributed to the environment in which national discussions of health system reform were possible.[1]

Much grand rhetoric and commentary notwithstanding, there were three specific goals of health insurance market reforms: (1) to make health insurance premiums more stable; (2) to make health insurance markets stable and sustainable in the long run; and (3) to make health insurance more affordable for the sick. The hope, and promise by some advocates, was that accomplishing these goals simultaneously would enable health insurance coverage rates to increase without public program expansion or explicit and substantial public subsidies.

Within the simultaneous pursuit of these three goals, however, lay inherent tensions that this chapter will explore. The primary tension is between trying to facilitate low and stable premiums and markets while asking those in good health to pay higher premiums to subsidize those who are facing greater health risks. This is hard enough without underlying health cost growth, but is more problematic in high-cost eras, which may be why waves of cost growth often lead to demands for yet more "reform." The purpose of this chapter is to offer solutions to inherent contradictions by changing some of the ways we think about the goals and implement the tools of insurance market reform.

Why reforms passed

The need for premium and market stability at the time was palpable. Figure 10.1 shows time trends of premium inflation compared with workers' earnings and general inflation. Premiums are by far the most

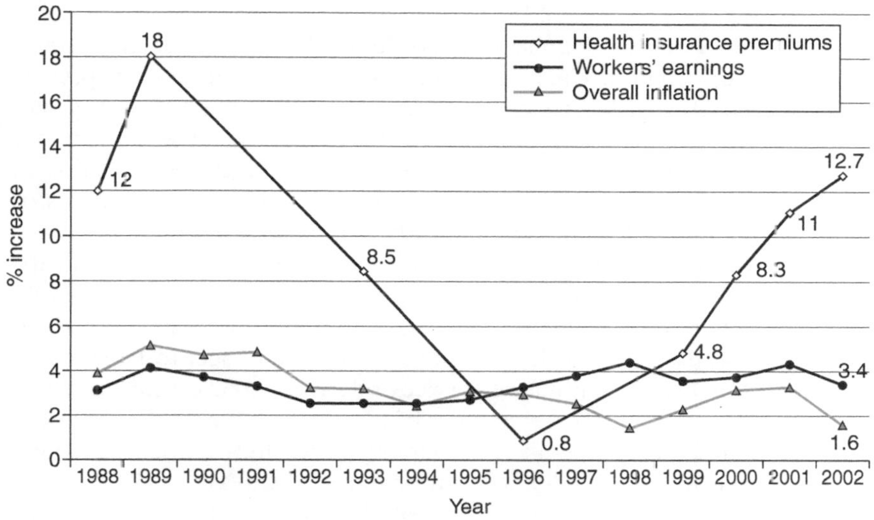

Figure 10.1 Increases in health insurance premiums compared with other indicators, 1988–2002. Data reflect the cost of premiums for a family of four.

Source: KFF/HRET Survey of Employer-sponsored Health Benefits, 1999, 2000, 2001, 2002; KPMG Survey of Employer-sponsored Health Benefits, 1988, 1993, 1996.

variable trend on the chart, with double-digit growth from 1988 to 1992 followed by declining and then very low growth followed by a rebound to recent experience with premium growth again outstripping general inflation and earnings by large margins. The bulk of state insurance reform legislative activity was between 1990 and 1992.

These premium trend data are for all firms. The Community Tracking Study's 1996–1997 survey of employers (Long and Marquis 1999) specifically asked about premium increases. Long and Marquis report just how much more likely small firms are to observe large increases in a given year. Comparing premium changes in 1996–1997 to other years in Figure 10.1, Long and Marquis report that that 23 percent of workers in firms with fewer than ten workers saw premiums increase more than 10 percent when average premium growth was at an all-time low, and when the average premium increase for all firms with fewer than ten workers was only 2.6 percent.

So premium stability was clearly a major goal of small-business advocates in the reform debates.[2] The corollary of high premium variance among small firms is that there is a much greater return to insurers from risk selection and underwriting in the small-group market than in the larger-group market. So regulations governing the rules of issue and insurer behavior were also necessary to achieve the objective of stability.

What reforms did (and did not) do

Other chapters in this volume provide detailed evidence on the effects of small-group (Simon, Chapter 2) and non-group (Chollet, Chapter 3) reforms, respectively. My conclusion from the evidence is that non-group reforms reduced coverage, small-group reforms had no effect on net coverage, and that the effect of each type of reform on the composition of insured risk pools is mixed or unknown. Studying the nuanced effects of reforms is complex, as both Simon and Chollet make clear.

Market reforms of any form create tradeoffs. Reforms that force insurers to increase the amount of risk pooling over what *laissez-faire* would generate – wherein the extent of risk segmentation is limited by nontrivial transaction costs – necessarily advantage those who expect to be sick and use large amounts of health care services relative to those who expect to be healthy (Nichols 2002). Since most of us expect to be healthy most of the time, market reforms – like risk pooling generally – amount to taxing the many a little to pay a lot to each of the few who get really sick. Of course, "many" and "a lot" are in the eye of the beholder, and when compared to alternative pricing structures that might be feasible, can appear innocuous or unacceptable to different people.

One way to sharpen this discussion is to write out a simplified version of how premiums (P) are actually set for small-group markets (assuming no real medical inflation over time for simplicity):

$$P = (1+L)[\alpha EXP_i + (1-\alpha)EXP_{group}]$$

Where L is the administrative load (in percentage terms), EXP_i represents the claims experience of the individual firms' workers in the past year or expected costs in future years, EXP_{group} is the claims experience of all firms in that firm's risk class (as defined by the insurer, and possibly constrained by state law), and $0 \leq \alpha \leq 1$. Pure experience rating would be the case of $\alpha = 1$, and pure community rating could be represented as $\alpha = 0$. Thus, the degree of importance of individual expected costs or claims experience – whether in the group or non-group markets – is a key barometer of how much pooling is taking place. Setting $\alpha = 0$ maximizes the stability of premiums over time, a major goal of insurance market reformers, but at the same time pure community rating can chase some healthy/low EXP_i groups or individuals out of the market by raising prices higher than their expected costs by too large a margin. Thus there is a tradeoff between stability of premiums and net coverage.

What about enforcement? Insurance contracts are complex, regulations that constrain them must therefore also be complex, and the spirit of complex regulations may be difficult to achieve. For example, consider rate bands. These are set to limit the variance or range of premiums an insurer can charge for the same policy, in essence, constraining variation across risk classes. Typically, they can be interpreted in the form of ±50 percent, which implies to many outside the insurance industry that the highest risks would pay no more than 50 percent above the average. But insurers are not required to set the "standard rate" – the rate charged to average risks – at the midpoint (or at any other specific point) of their premium ranges. In fact, many of them set the standard rate at or very near the bottom of their desired premium range. So, in fact, a ±50 percent rate band can be used to charge high risks double the "standard" rate (Hall 2000/2001). This may be actuarially appropriate, or closer to it than the rate band tried to allow, but the point is that there may be considerable leeway to deviate from the spirit of the rate band regulation.

States generally have two lines of defense when it comes to enforcement.[3] The first is that each licensed insurer has an actuary sign a statement that indicates the company's practice and prices are in compliance with state law. This links the chief actuary's professional ethics and good standing within the profession with the company's behavior. The general belief within the regulatory community is that this is enough to ensure actual compliance for most insurers.

The second enforcement mechanism is the examination audit, not unlike a bank audit, in which Insurance Department examiners visit insurer headquarters and examine all offers and in-force contracts. This is fairly rare, and is increasingly triggered only by complaints. There is some doubt about the effectiveness of complaint triggers, for the basic question is, who would complain? No firm receiving a very low premium offer would complain, nor would those receiving a high one easily know that another firm got an "illegally" low offer on the same policy form. Agents and brokers might complain on behalf of certain clients, but this would not endear them to the accused insurer, and the path of least resistance may be to find their important clients another policy from another insurer. Thus, some insurers may expect the probability of being caught violating rate bands to be very low and may not have actually changed pricing behavior post-reform. In addition, some state laws permit out-of-state carriers to issue policies through state associations, and this effectively skirts prohibitions on re-underwriting, for example (Grollier 2002). All this plus the "looser than intended" rate bands described by Mark Hall (2000/2001) may have contributed to the measured "effects" of reform being relatively difficult to discern.

But assuming that compliance is high owing to actuarial ethics and that enforcement is effective (and with enough data collection and auditing activity it surely could be), I now turn to the tradeoffs inherent to each specific set of market reforms.

Limits on pre-existing condition exclusions

Most policies impose waiting and look-back periods to prevent people from buying insurance once they discover a health problem. If waiting periods differ, the policy with the most generous (shortest) waiting period would always attract the sickest people, *ceteris paribus*, so it is actually efficient to standardize the lengths for all policies, else the equilibrium pre-existing condition clause could be quite long. At the same time, forcing the waiting period to be too short increases the risk of allowing those with high risks to take advantage of the voluntary purchase system. Thus, even in this least objectionable form of regulation, there is a tradeoff involved between lower premiums for most and access for the least healthy.

Guaranteed renewal

Guaranteed renewal rules prevent an insurer from refusing to sell to the same person again after they have been found to be quite sick. This is the flip side of using pre-existing condition exclusions to prevent people from buying only after they discover they are sick. Again, in the absence of regulation, insurers could offer lower premiums without this provision, and no firm offering guaranteed renewal on a voluntary basis could sustain low premiums if other insurers did not also include it in their policy offers. Forcing all insurers to guarantee renewal (not necessarily at last year's prices) is similar to forcing them to limit their pre-existing condition waiting and look-back periods. It adds something probably small to costs while offering quite a bit of peace of mind to those whose fate is tragic.

Guaranteed renewal does interact with the absence of guaranteed issue in the following possibly problematic way. With guaranteed renewal laws alone, some insurers have been reported to close books of business or specific policy forms they have sold in the past, offer the healthiest in that pool (and only them) a new product at substantially lower rates, and then claim – technically correctly – that the risk pool in the surviving closed product merits extremely high premium increases, ultimately chasing even the sickest enrollees away because they cannot afford the premium (Terhune 2002). It is hard to know how often this occurs, but it clearly violates the sprit of guaranteed renewal law, and the many regulators are trying to stop it (Patel and Pauly 2002).

Guaranteed issue

Guaranteed issue means that insurers cannot refuse to sell to any applicant, regardless of health status. Without restrictions on premium variance, however, they can always price any product beyond the reach of most Americans and thereby protect their existing (underwritten) risk pools. Guaranteed issue laws often were applied to one or a few products, a situation analytically similar to guaranteed renewal without guaranteed issue: the good risks can be segmented into nonguaranteed issue products, reserving the guaranteed issue products for bad risks only, and pooling is thus still minimized. Guaranteed issue of *all* products, as the 1996 Health Insurance Portability and Accountability Act required in the small-group market, is the only way around these effective segmentation strategies, and that is the one type of guaranteed issue that actually engenders pooling and thereby raises premiums for those who were able to purchase low-cost policies without guaranteed issue. In essence, all product guaranteed issue is a gentle form of community rating, wherein all those enrolled in the same policy form and risk class would be charged the same amount.

In a sense, guaranteed issue makes insurers adapt their underwriting strategies from weeding out those they do not want to sell to determining at what price they want to offer the same product to different types of people, and how many different explicitly priced categories of people – risk classes – they want to maintain. One important but unanswered question is the extent to which insurers implicitly pool and cross-subsidize different risk classes within their insured base across product lines. Some empirical work indicates that the amount of implicit pooling, even within the non-group market where guaranteed issue is fairly rare, is quite substantial (Pauly and Herring 1999), and the amount of implicit risk pooling within employer-sponsored health insurance, where guaranteed issue is virtually universal now, is well known to be considerable (Monheit *et al.* 1995/1996). Thus, the very healthy could find a better deal as long as they remain healthy in more fully underwritten markets.

Premium variance restrictions

The most invasive technique to force risk pooling on private agents – those who voluntarily purchase insurance and the insurers who sell to them – is to limit the variance in premiums insurers may use for the same policy form. Pure community rating is the simplest approach and permits no variance, but it is also fairly rare. Much more common are modified community rating statutes – wherein specific dimensions, e.g., health status age, gender, or location – are used to set differential prices. In addition, many states constrain premium variance through the use of rate bands, which typically limit the ratio of highest and lowest premiums for a given form to 3:1 (±50 percent) or 4:1 (±60 percent) regardless of risk factors that may be allowed to justify the premiums offered. Again, any binding constraint on premium variance forces the insured – through the middleman of insurers – to transfer expected expenditures from the healthy to the sick. This naturally leads some healthy to decline coverage, but also provides access to lower-cost products than would otherwise be available to higher risks, the classic tradeoff in insurance market reforms.

Sharing risk more broadly

The fundamental difficulty with using such regulations to accomplish social goals in the group and in the non-group markets is that there are potentially many losers: people who have to pay more after regulation than before, perhaps even a majority. Furthermore, the success of regulation ultimately hinges upon using legal constraints to force private companies to make choices they would not otherwise make, so that incentives to frustrate the goals of regulations are endemic. The purpose of this chapter is to offer a solution that is "outside the box" of past and existing regulations and devise a creative way to accomplish our common goals with less economic loss or distortion created in insurance markets than we have generated in the past. This solution could apply to group and non-group markets alike.

More detail on many elements of the policy proposal I will offer for consideration is contained in two papers I have coauthored with Urban Institute health economists (Holahan *et al.* 2001, 2003). This section and chapter will more fully develop the theory and analytics underlying the risk-spreading core of that proposal.

The basic "new" idea is to subsidize those with excess health risk in addition to those with low incomes in their pursuit of health insurance. At present the nation subsidizes the elderly and some severely disabled with Medicare and the very low-income plus children and certain very sick individuals through Medicaid. We also subsidize the bulk of the non-elderly population in proportion to their income tax rates (i.e., regressively) through the employer premium contribution exemption from individual income taxes. In addition, the federal tax code subsidizes the self-employed, a relatively high-income group, again in proportion to their marginal tax rates, but no one else is subsidized at the present time in the non-group market.

By contrast, we pointedly do not subsidize many poor individuals – Medicaid only covers about 50 percent of those with incomes below poverty – nor do we subsidize many near-poor households who are less likely to have employer-sponsored insurance offered to them or are less likely to afford the out-of-pocket premiums required from employer-offered coverage. Finally, high-risk pools, in the thirty states where they exist, transfer implicit subsidies from the premium taxes levied on non-group insurers – and largely paid by non-group insurance purchasers with inelastic demand – to some individuals who have been denied health insurance and who choose to buy into the high risk at subsidized but still high premiums. High-risk pool enrollees, about 150,000 nationwide, turn out to be a very small fraction of the 1 percent of the population that might be eligible (2.8 million) by virtue of having been denied insurance by a *bona fide* insurer. Except for these enrollees, there are no explicit subsidies for high-risk individuals in the United States, unless they are sick enough to be declared disabled under Social Security or Medicaid law.

So we currently share risk inefficiently and with substantial inequities, and consequently, we still manage to leave over 40 million people uninsured despite considerable federal and state funds devoted to health insurance subsidies. Many of the uninsured are relatively healthy (Pauly and Nichols 2002), but some are not, and they are the ones most in need of risk-based subsidies.

Figure 10.2 illustrates the basic concepts of how insurance markets might work under different pricing and subsidy regimes. Imagine that individuals are arrayed in ascending order of their individual expected health care costs (E[c]). Let V(HI) be the hypothetical value of health insurance to the individual, a proxy for willingness to pay, and note that Figure 10.2 embodies the assumption that V(HI) is increasing like E[c] but not at the same rate, partially owing to income constraints among the sickest and highest-risk individuals.

If insurance were priced at individually underwritten prices, i.e., if all people or groups were offered a policy at a price equal to their expected health care costs (I abstract from insurance loading factors for simplicity),

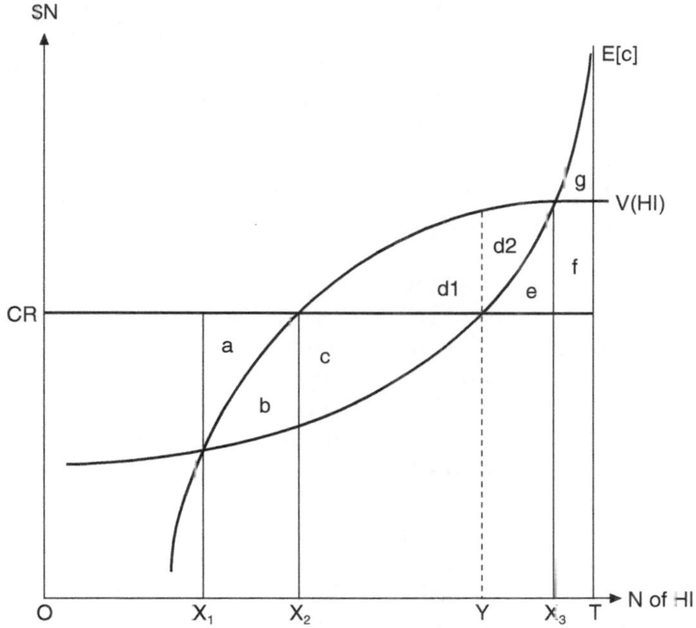

Figure 10.2 Distributions of the cost and value of insurance.

Source: Author's hypothetical, wherein people are arrayed along the horizontal axis in ascending order of their expected health care costs, E[c], which are presumed to be positively correlated (but not perfectly) with their willingness to pay for health insurance, V(HI).

risk-averse people would purchase the policy if and only if $V(HI) \geq E[c]$. In that case, in the terms of Figure 10.2, the uninsured would number X_1 plus $T - X_3$ and the voluntarily insured buyers would be $X_3 - X_1$. Economic welfare or aggregate consumer surplus, the integral of the difference between willingness to pay and expected cost, would equal the sum of areas $b + c + d1 + d2$.

In the polar opposite case of regulated community rating as the pricing rule, all policies would be offered at CR, buyers would be those for whom $V(HI) \geq CR$, the number of uninsured would change to X_2 while economic welfare would be $d1 + d2 + e + f - g$. At a minimum, community rating (or any regulation, generally, that forces more risk pooling than *laissez-faire* entails) helps the highest risk afford coverage; as drawn $T - X_3$ would gain coverage if the price were limited to CR. However, this gain comes at the cost of some people dropping coverage when faced with the higher community rate ($X_2 - X_1$), as well as redistribution of economic welfare, since area b is lost by $X_2 - X_1$, area c is lost by $Y - X_2$, and while $e + f$ is gained by $T - Y$, g must be financed somehow from the members of the society or "community" of insured people. In pure community rating schemes, g is financed out of the area c lost by $Y - X_2$, that is, purchasers who still buy at CR (but who could have bought for less under *laissez-faire*) effectively subsidize the high risk, and the insurer plays the part of the broker or middleman in that cross-subsidization. In effect, community rating gives insurers the right and duty to collect a kind of producers' surplus from $Y - X_2$ which is then "spent" on $T - X_3$. Whether c and g are equal in value for each insurer is of course an empirical question, and predictions about their equivalence or likely inequality may lead to instability in the CR or withdrawal from the market by commercial insurers, both of which have been observed where regulations have been imposed.[4]

The new idea here is for a "third way" to guide pricing and subsidy eligibility in insurance markets. The core of the idea has two elements: let those who can buy cheaper than the community rate purchase insurance free of price regulations, and subsidize those who cannot, so that no one pays more than the community rate. The risk spreading concept is to broaden the "tax base" beyond the people between Y and X_2 to the entire society, thus using general taxation to finance area g. The coverage- and economic welfare-enhancing impact of this approach, compared to community rating, is apparent by noticing that $X_2 - X_1$ will purchase insurance again, as under *laissez-faire*, and $T - Y$ are made no worse off than under community rating. Thus, spreading risk-based subsidies over the entire population and allowing actuarially fair pricing where it is feasibly below the equilibrium community rate clearly dominates taxing healthy buyers to finance care for sick buyers as community rating does, *assuming the population at large agrees to pay the general taxes required.*

This is of course a nontrivial political assumption, but it is necessary for the risk-based subsidy idea to come to fruition. The power of the analytic example is to show that net economic welfare would be enhanced by risk-based subsidies over community rating. Thus *if* a society were using a form of community rating now, and I argued above that all insurance reforms are just different degrees of community rating in the important sense of forced risk pooling, *then* moving to a risk-based subsidy approach would likely be a good idea. But if a society were still comfortable with *laissez-faire*, then adopting a risk-based subsidy scheme might represent a more dubious tradeoff. Table 10.1 summarizes the analytic results comparing *laissez-faire*, community rating, and risk-based subsidies assuming the E[c] and V(HI) functions are similar to the shapes depicted in Figure 10.2.

Empirical techniques

To approximate the empirical reality behind these analytic results, I estimated an E[c] function using 2000 MEPS data. I used the sample of non-elderly adults (18–64) with private insurance (group and non-group) to abstract away from moral hazard issues that would have been important if I had included the uninsured or public program enrollees. Those with private insurance comprise the vast majority of US residents, but not all, yet are still broadly representative of the general population in terms of health care cost distributions (Berk and Monheit 2001). I employed a standard two-part model, wherein the first stage estimates a probit on the probability of having some expense in the year, and then the second stage estimates the natural log of expenditures, conditional on having positive expenditures. Errors from the second stage were smeared to facilitate transformations of predictions back into actual dollars according to the methods developed by Duan *et al.* (1983).

Expected expense for each individual adult was calculated as the product of the probability of having positive expense and the predicted expenditure level, given that individual's characteristics. Individuals without positive expenses were attributed expected expenses based on the model that was estimated on those with positive expense. All adults had some probability of nonzero expense (minimum probability of 0.37) and

Table 10.1 Analytic results under different pricing and subsidy regimes

Regime	*Uninsured*	*Net economic welfare*	*"Loss" implicitly redistributed*
Laissez-faire	$X_1 + T - X_3$	b + c + d1 + d2	
Community rating	X_2	d1 + d2 + e + f − g	g
Risk-based subsidies	X_1	b + c + d1 + d2 + e + f − g	g

the minimum predicted logarithm of expense conditional on some expense is nontrivial (minimum predicted natural logarithm of 5.18), so all adults have some positive expected expense. Descriptive statistics on these distributions and predictions are shown in Table 10.3. Empirically, the distribution of E[c] is clearly increasing at an increasing rate as we move from minimum to maximum value, as drawn in Figure 10.2. Explanatory variables in the two-part model included age, gender, race/ethnicity, education, marital status, parental status, urban location, census region, work status, health status (fair or poor subjective overall health assessment, presence of a chronic condition), and income (poverty category). Complete results of the two-part model estimation are available in Appendix 10.1.

One interesting methodological question is, what can serve as an estimate of V(HI) to facilitate measurement of the welfare analysis analogous to Figure 10.2? This is more difficult than estimating E[c] since V(HI) and economic welfare include not only observed willingness to pay, revealed by the transaction or demand price, but also the consumer surplus from buying insurance at the observed price. Thankfully, the point of this chapter is not to estimate V(HI), but rather to compare the welfare results of alternative pricing/regulatory regimes. Thus, given a conventional estimate of the E[c] function, it will suffice for our purposes to use a *plausible* V(HI) function and simply compare the number of uninsured and proximate economic welfare calculations under competing pricing regimes, assuming that the same stable V(HI) *function* holds in all cases. Letting Y = household income and E[c] be final predicted expense from the two-part model for all privately insured non-elderly adults, I used

$$V(HI) = \min.\ (0.3*Y,\ a*E[c] + 0.5*Y^{3/4})$$

Several assumptions underlie this particular V(HI). First, I assume that no person would spend more than 30 percent of household income on

Table 10.2 Predicted expenditures for non-elderly adults covered by private insurance

Variables	*Min.*	*Max.*	*Mean*	*Median*	*Mode*
Predicted log of expenditures	5.18	9.01	6.60	6.45	6.11
Probability expenditures > 0	0.37	1.00	0.87	0.89	0.83
Predicted expenditures (E[c])	189.73	20,338.74	2,299.57	1,419.45	927.46
Value of health insurance (V(HI))	0.00	62,377.20	3,677.23	3,159.53	0.00

Source: 2000 Medical Expenditure Panel Survey.

Note
Weighted basic statistics on constructed expenditure variables.

health insurance. Second, V(HI) is increasing in predicted expense and in income, but in income at a concave or decreasing rate, to reflect the assumption of declining relative risk aversion. Finally, the gross importance of income in the value function is itself a function of income, since $a = 0.7$ if income is greater than four times the federal poverty line, $a = 0.6$ if income is between two and four times the poverty line, 0.4 if income is between the poverty line and two times the poverty line, and 0.3 if income is below poverty. This reflects an assumption that higher-income people are more likely to be willing to buy insurance to cover a greater share of their expected expense than lower-income people, *ceteris paribus*.

The V(HI) function is closest in concept to a "risk premium" amount a person is willing to pay for insurance in the classic economic theory of uncertainty and demand for insurance (Laffont 1989). Using mean values of V(HI) as calculated and the variance of health expenditures as observed, the corresponding value of absolute risk aversion for my sample is −0.000165. This is smaller than most conventional estimates of risk aversion (Feldman and Dowd 1991), so at a minimum we may conclude this form of the V(HI) function is not biasing the insurance decision toward purchasing.

Empirical results

Table 10.3 reports the empirical results from calculating the analytic concepts illustrated in Figure 10.2 with the estimated E[c] and assumed V(HI). In column 1, we see that community rating would lead to twice as much uninsurance as *laissez-faire*, and that the risk-based subsidy approach would almost bring about universal coverage. The last result must mean that the number of people who do not buy insurance because they have very low value for it, i.e., people for whom $V(HI) < E[c] < CR$, i.e., X_1 in Figure 10.2, is only 4 percent of the population. The superior coverage performance of the risk-based subsidy scheme compared to community rating also suggests that $X_2 - X_1$, the number of people who would buy under actuarial pricing who would not buy under community rating, is large.

Table 10.3 Empirical results under different pricing and subsidy regimes

Regime	*% uninsured*	*Net economic welfare ($ billion)*	*"Loss" implicitly redistributed ($ billion)*
Laissez-faire	13.76	165.7	
Community rating	27.96	121.6	17.4
Risk-based subsidies	4.09	148.3	17.4

The economic welfare calculations illustrate the nature of health policy tradeoffs nicely. *Laissez-faire* does best, followed by risk-based subsidies, followed by the less efficient attempt to spread risk, community rating. *Laissez-faire* does best because no "losses" like the area g have to be financed or redistributed. In other words, *laissez-faire* is more efficient in economic terms but risk-based subsidies and community rating have a different kind of equity to counterbalance their reduced efficiency. Risk spreading transfers welfare to the higher risk. Which kind of society and scheme would you rather live in? That is the first question policymakers must answer.

But the key second question, which is really the question for this chapter, might be, if enough members of society agree that the equity distribution in *laissez-faire* is unacceptable, is there an alternative to traditional insurance market reforms that might be welfare-enhancing? The results of the risk-based subsidy approach are fairly encouraging on this score, since spreading risk beyond the insured in a community rating/insurance market regulation context *and* permitting actuarial-based pricing in a large segment of the market would apparently both reduce the number of uninsured considerably and increase economic welfare by roughly 20 percent ((148.3 − 121.6)/(121.6 + 148.3)/2) under plausible estimates of expected cost and value of health insurance distributions. Thus, there are alternatives to substantial regulation that may simultaneously improve equity of access to health insurance, promote genuine stability in insurance markets, and increase coverage at minimum economic cost to the society at large. Of course, minimum economic cost does not mean that the public subsidy cost would be small compared to today's level of commitment. Preliminary simulation evidence suggests that risk-based subsidies alone (ignoring income-based subsidies, which might also be desirable) would require approximately $50 billion in new public moneys in 2002 dollars (Holahan *et al.* 2003). This may be beyond current social willingness to pay, but it is hardly beyond the realm of imagination in a $10 trillion economy and a $2.2 trillion federal budget.

Conclusions

Insurance market reforms were passed for good reasons but have proven less effective than advocates hoped at accomplishing our basic social goals of increasing coverage in total or at least for the higher risk among us. This chapter has offered some analytic and empirical results which suggest there may be a better way to increase coverage at lower net economic cost by spreading the risk of higher-risk individuals over a broader pool than their copurchasers in a community rating context, while allowing the majority for whom actuarial prices are relatively low to continue to purchase insurance in a relatively unregulated environment. Our collective willingness to finance these risk-based subsidies of course remains a major issue, in that *laissez-faire* will always yield higher economic welfare in the technical economists' framework. But if the relative value of greater equity of access for the most needy among us – those with high expected health costs – exceeds as little as 10 percent of total economic welfare under *laissez-faire*, under quite plausible assumptions then net welfare can be enhanced by choosing risk-based subsidies over community rating-type market reform regulations. In other words, targeted subsidies broadly financed, partly by allowing the healthy to buy insurance as cheap as they could unpooled, may be much more efficient than broader subsidies more narrowly financed by implicit taxes on the healthy alone. This is a result that current and future policymakers may find it fruitful to consider.

Appendix 10.1 Results of a two-part model of health expenditures

Table 10.4 First stage regression: probit estimate of the likelihood of incurring positive expenditures

Variable	*Coefficient*	*Std err.*	*t*	*P>t*	*[95% conf. interval]*	
Age 25–45	0.0943196	0.082	1.15	0.251	0.0673104	0.25595
Age 46–54	0.1734805	0.091	1.91	0.058	0.0056364	0.35260
Age 55–64	0.1840716	0.103	1.79	0.075	0.0188952	0.38704
Female	0.6047441	0.046	13.21	0.000	0.5144436	0.69504
Hispanic	0.3737313	0.076	4.89	0.000	0.5243801	0.22308
Black	0.4577338	0.075	6.14	0.000	0.6048750	0.31059
Other race	0.4180949	0.134	3.12	0.002	0.6827478	0.15344
Some college	0.2457897	0.059	4.13	0.000	0.1284988	0.36308
College or more	0.4824966	0.072	6.72	0.000	0.3408081	0.62419
Married	0.0858757	0.051	1.69	0.094	0.0146493	0.18640
Parent	0.0540956	0.060	0.91	0.365	0.1716217	0.06343
Urban	0.0430004	0.064	0.67	0.504	0.0838219	0.16982
Reside in Midwest	0.0422438	0.068	0.62	0.537	0.0923317	0.17682
Reside in south	0.0438938	0.066	0.67	0.505	0.1735000	0.08571
Reside in west	0.0297319	0.110	0.27	0.787	0.1874758	0.24694
Working	0.2676511	0.064	4.20	0.000	0.3934496	0.14185
Fair or poor health	0.4646375	0.118	3.94	0.000	0.2317792	0.69750
Has chronic condition	2.3740330	0.242	9.81	0.000	1.8968560	2.85121
Income = 2 to 3× poverty	0.1261804	0.127	1.00	0.321	0.1237525	0.37611
Income = 3 to 4× poverty	0.0711173	0.120	0.59	0.553	0.1647480	0.30698
Income ≥ 4× poverty	0.1709513	0.116	1.47	0.142	0.0578314	0.39973
Constant	0.4384583	0.133	3.29	0.001	0.1754093	0.70151

Note
N = 9,592. Overall F (21,168) = 25.79.

Table 10.5 Ordinary least squares estimates of health care expenditures for persons with positive expenditures

Variable	*Coefficient*	*Std err.*	*t*	*P>t*	*[95% conf. interval]*	
Age 25–45	0.2022777	0.0717803	2.82	0.005	0.0606793	0.3438760
Age 46–54	0.4026362	0.0743797	5.41	0.000	0.2559101	0.5493623
Age 55–64	0.4623737	0.0682640	6.77	0.000	0.3277118	0.5970355
Female	0.4499465	0.0358337	12.56	0.000	0.3792588	0.5206342
Hispanic	0.2926658	0.0583730	5.01	0.000	0.4078161	0.1775154
Black	0.2332770	0.0587200	3.97	0.000	0.3491118	0.1174422
Other race	0.2849977	0.1140041	2.50	0.013	0.5098893	0.6010610
Some college	0.0833607	0.0432021	1.93	0.055	0.0018624	0.1685838
College or more	0.1823569	0.0457535	3.99	0.000	0.0921006	0.2726131
Married	0.1108242	0.0479591	2.31	0.022	0.0162170	0.2054314
Parent	0.0544325	0.0387978	1.40	0.162	0.1309675	0.0221026
Urban	0.0046508	0.0591979	0.08	0.937	0.1214282	0.1121267
Reside in Midwest	0.0748764	0.0578907	1.29	0.197	0.1890753	0.0393225
Reside in south	0.0509981	0.0620929	0.82	0.413	0.1734865	0.0714903
Reside in west	0.0410666	0.0686712	0.60	0.551	0.1765318	0.0943985
Working	0.3130395	0.0455970	6.87	0.000	0.4029871	0.2230919
Fair or poor health	0.8414268	0.0575719	14.62	0.000	0.7278569	0.9549967
Has chronic condition	0.9711947	0.0380880	25.50	0.000	0.8960600	1.0463290
Income = 2 to 3× poverty	0.0366736	0.1440586	0.25	0.799	0.3208527	0.2475054
Income = 3 to 4× poverty	0.0079104	0.1274161	0.06	0.951	0.2434386	0.2592594
Income ≥ 4× poverty	0.1117795	0.1349309	0.83	0.408	0.1543935	0.3779526
Constant	5.9212540	0.1429828	41.41	0.000	5.6391970	6.2033100

Note
N = 8,144. Overall F (21,168) = 141.73.

Acknowledgments

I am grateful to Alan Monheit for many helpful comments on an earlier version, to Gigi Liu for research assistance and to Cindy Saintz-Martinez for programming assistance. All errors and opinions expressed herein are my sole responsibility.

Notes

1 See *Health Affairs*, spring I (1994), for a wide range of views of the need for national reform at that time.
2 Note that these data are for the period *after* reforms had been implemented in most states. In fact, the variance experience of small firms was far worse in the 1988–1992 period.
3 I am grateful to Mary Beth Senkewicz of the National Association of Insurance Commissioners for helpful discussions on enforcement.
4 CR under community rating will have to adjust for the dropping by $X_2 - X_1$, for a true population average E[c] is not sustainable in a voluntary purchase

environment; the actual CR will be higher than the population average. I have drawn Figure 10.2 assuming the final sustainable equilibrium community rate is CR. In real life few true death spirals have ever been observed, so such an equilibrium probably exists in most circumstances though individual insurers do exist and average premiums do rise when community rating is imposed, to be sure.

References

Berk, M. and Monheit, A. (2001) "The Concentration of Health Care Expenditures, Revisited." *Health Affairs*, 20 (2): 9–18.

Duan, N., Manning, W.G., Morris, C.N., and Newhouse, J.P. (1983) "Consistent Estimation of the Demand for Health Services." *Journal of Business and Economic Statistics*, 1: 115–126.

Feldman, R. and Dowd, B. (1991) "A New Estimate of the Welfare Loss of Health Insurance." *American Economic Review*, 81: 297–301.

Grollier, G. (2002) "Some Insurers raise rates on Sickest: Regulators are trying to stop Reunderwriting of Health Policies." *Orlando Sentinel*, August 11.

Hall, M. (2001/2002) "The Structure and Enforcement of Health Insurance Rating Reforms." *Inquiry*, 37: 376–388.

Holahan, J., Nichols, L., and Blumberg, L. (2001) "Expanding Health Insurance Coverage: A New Federal/State Approach" in Jack A. Meyer and Elliot Wicks (eds), *Covering America: Real Remedies for the Uninsured*. Washington, DC: Economic and Social Research Institute. Available from: www.esresearch.org.

Holahan, J., Nichols, L., Blumberg, L., and Chen, Y.-C. (2003) "A New Approach to Risk Spreading via Coverage–Expansion Subsidies." *American Economic Review*, 93 (2): 277–282.

Laffont, J.-J. (1989) *The Economics of Uncertainty and Information*. Cambridge MA: MIT Press.

Long, S.H. and Marquis, M.S. (1999) "Stability and Variation in Employment-based Health Insurance, 1995–1997." *Health Affairs*, 18 (6): 133–139.

Monheit, A., Nichols, L., and Selden, T. (1995/1996) "How are Net Health Insurance Benefits Distributed in the Employment-related Insurance Market?" *Inquiry*, 32 (4): 379–391.

Nichols, L. (2000) "State Regulation: What Have We Learned So Far?" *Journal of Health Politics, Policy and Law*, 25 (1): 175–196.

Nichols, L. and Blumberg, L. (1998) "A Different Kind of New Federalism? The Health Insurance Portability and Accountability Act." *Health Affairs*, 17 (3): 25–42.

Patel, V. and Pauly, M. (2002) "Guaranteed Renewability and the Problem of Risk Variation in the Individual Insurance Market." *Health Affairs* (Web Exclusives), August 28.

Pauly, M. and Herring, B. (1999) *Pooling Insurance Risks*. Washington, DC: American Enterprise Institute.

Pauly, M. and Nichols, L. (2002) "The Non-group Insurance Market: Short on Fact, Long on Opinions and Policy Disputes." *Health Affairs* (Web Exclusives), October 23.

Terhune, C. (2002) "Health Insurer's Premium Practices Add to Profit Surge, Roil Customers." *Wall Street Journal*, April 9.

US General Accounting Office (1992) "Access to Health Insurance Regulations: State Efforts to Assist Small Businesses." GAO-HRD-92-90.

11 Insurance market reform

When, how, and why?

Katherine Swartz

There is wide variation in the extent to which insurance companies and managed care companies (hereafter collectively referred to as carriers) are regulated by states. Until the early 1980s, states with greater regulation of health insurance markets did so in a way that often mirrored regulation of public utilities – i.e., state commissioners of insurance or insurance departments focused their attention on justifications of rate increases and the financial reserves of the carriers. But over the 1980s and 1990s a number of states used their regulatory powers to try to assure more people access to health insurance either by restricting rate setting based on people's characteristics (chiefly medical conditions and age) or by requiring carriers to accept all applicants or renew policies for existing enrollees. The use of these regulations raises several questions. When is it appropriate to introduce regulatory reform to health insurance markets? How can states create effective reforms, and what standards should be used to measure effectiveness? Why might regulations of health insurance markets be good policy instruments?

In what follows, I address these questions in the context of the non-group (or individual) health insurance markets, although much of what I argue applies to the small-group markets, too. In the next section I focus on when it is appropriate to intervene in health insurance markets. As part of this, I discuss two conditions that are sources of market failure in non-group and small-group health insurance markets. Then I briefly describe the forms of competition between carriers in these insurance markets and why such competition reflects market failure in these markets. The outcome of this competition does not permit full access to health insurance for many people. In the third section I outline how government might intervene in the non-group and small-group health insurance markets so as to address the market failure. In particular, I describe a proposal to have government act as reinsurer in these markets and take primary responsibility for the expenses of extremely high-cost people in any one year. In the fourth section, I discuss why government should focus its regulatory efforts on addressing sources of market failure rather than simply trying to "level the playing field." As part of this discussion, I describe lessons learned from states' use of regulations since 1990. I also describe the tradeoff between providing people with more choice and lower premiums. I conclude with a brief discussion of the implications for policymakers of trying to bolster the non-group and small-group insurance markets in order to reduce the number of uninsured.

When should we intervene in insurance markets?

Economic theory offers two justifications for government intervention in the economy and markets. The first involves redistributing resources so as to assist poor or otherwise deserving groups of people who are unable to afford goods (like food or health care) that are deemed to be necessities. Economists argue that such resource redistributions should take place outside the market in order to leave the market's efficiency-enhancing incentives as intact as possible. This argument, for example, prefers a direct income transfer like food stamps to a policy of controls on the prices of food.[1] The second justification for intervention in a market involves redressing causes of market failures – conditions of various kinds that result in a failure by a market to achieve economic efficiency. Markets fail to achieve economic efficiency when at least one of the following four conditions is present: sellers or buyers have market power (i.e., they have some power to set prices); production or consumption of the product creates negative or positive externalities (e.g., pollution is a negative externality when it has costs that are not charged to the producer of the pollution); the product is a public good (i.e., a good that cannot be created only for people who pay for it); and asymmetric or imperfect information exists in the market.

In the case of health insurance, asymmetric information prevents non-group and small-group markets from being competitive. In most markets, when consumers and producers do not have the same information, the information asymmetry generally favors producers because consumers have difficulty determining all of a product's characteristics. In health insurance markets information asymmetry favors consumers. Consumers know far more about why they wish to purchase health insurance than carriers can ever know. Carriers know from experience that people who know or suspect they will have expensive health care needs in the coming year are also more likely to apply for insurance coverage. Such people make up a disproportionate fraction of the people who apply for coverage every year. However, the carriers cannot identify who these people are because they do not have full information with which to correctly distinguish between applicants who have high probabilities and those who have low probabilities of using high-cost medical care. This creates an adverse selection problem.

Carriers fear adverse selection with good reason. If they cannot accurately predict the expenses of a group of insured people, they run the risk of losses and going out of business. As a result, explained more fully in the next section, instead of competing on the price of insurance (the premium), carriers compete in terms of mechanisms to screen out people they expect will use high-cost care – people who are sometimes referred to as high risk. Competition with respect to mechanisms to screen out high-risk people yields inefficiency in health insurance markets because the carriers spend resources on activities that do not produce insurance *per se*. These selection activities cause people perceived to be high risk to have less access to health insurance than do lower-risk people – some because they are denied coverage outright and some because they are offered coverage only at very high premiums. The very high premiums are an effective method of dissuading high-risk people from purchasing coverage.

Thus, government intervention in the non-group (and small-group) insurance markets can be justified because the asymmetric information that exists in these markets prevents carriers from competing on the basis of price and quality. Equally important, having identified asymmetric information as the underlying cause of market failure within non-group insurance markets, appropriate government actions to address the cause of the market failure can be crafted.

Competition in health insurance markets

Health insurance is sold in three interconnected markets. We can loosely distinguish between large employer-group, small-group, and individual (or non-group) insurance markets. Some carriers actively sell coverage in all three markets but most do not. More often, we observe large carriers selling coverage to large-employer groups, and smaller carriers selling in the small-group and individual markets. In addition to these three types of markets, every state (and the District of Columbia) regulates how insurance is sold within its borders. The states have different regulations governing facets of insurance ranging from what benefits must be covered by insurance policies to how rates are determined to requirements about financial reserves.[2] As a result, there are fifty-one different submarkets within each of the three distinct markets. Many carriers, particularly smaller carriers, offer policies only in those states with similar regulations so they do not have to keep track of and respond to many regulatory changes. One result of this is that, in the individual markets in 1997, the number of carriers selling individual policies ranged from only two or three (in Delaware, Idaho, and Alaska) to more than forty (in New York and Texas) (Chollet *et al.* 2000). In 1997, just under 700 carriers sold individual policies in the United States; by comparison, 2,450 carriers sold policies in the large- and small-group markets (Chollet *et al.* 2000). In spite of this difference, the individual and group markets are characterized by a small number of carriers having at least half of the total number of policies sold in each type of market in each state (Chollet *et al.* 2000).

Health coverage is sold and priced quite differently in the three types of health insurance markets (ignoring for the moment the fifty-one different jurisdictions' regulations). The selling practices and pricing differences largely reflect the extent to which carriers fear adverse selection in each of the markets. In the large-group market, adverse selection at the group level is uncommon since almost all employees in a large employer enroll for coverage. (If an employer offers a choice of plans, then carriers may be concerned about adverse selection if they are the choice of a small proportion of the group.) Employees and their dependents in large groups pay average premiums based on the total expected costs of the group; a particular person's expected medical care costs are not factored into the premium he or she pays. Usually, the employer also negotiates with several carriers as to the out-of-pocket cost sharing and benefits covered, and makes tradeoffs between these aspects of the policy and the premiums.

Small groups (typically, groups with less than fifty employees) and individuals face very different markets. Per policy, premiums are substantially higher in these markets than in the large-group market; it is not unusual to find premiums for single or family policies to be more than twice as expensive for small groups or individuals, compared with those in large groups. The primary reason for these higher premiums is that pooling of risks occurs over much smaller groups of people in the small-group and individual markets. As a result, the variance in the expected costs is much larger than that found in the large-group policies. This in turn translates to a greater risk that actual costs will exceed expected costs in the non-group and small-group markets. Carriers respond to this risk in two ways. First, they set higher premiums for small-group and non-group policies because they need to be compensated for bearing greater risk. Second, they try to insure only people who they expect will have lower medical costs; they try to avoid insuring people whom they perceive to be high-cost users of medical care. Carriers go to great expense to selectively insure people who have low risks of high medical care costs – sometimes referred to as low-risk people. The costs of the risk-selection mechanisms used by carriers are a non-trivial component of the higher premiums for small-group and individual policies.

Information asymmetry shapes the form of competition between carriers

Carriers cannot tell for sure from applicant information whether an applicant will have high medical care use in the coming year. But as noted earlier, they believe that a disproportionate share of people who apply for insurance coverage consists of individuals who expect to have high medical care use in the near future – perhaps because a close relative has had a medical condition or because they themselves have had a medical problem in the past. The problem for carriers is that they usually cannot obtain this information; there is an asymmetry of information between what the carriers know and what the insurance applicants know. As we also noted earlier, when there is asymmetric information in a market, the market fails to achieve economic efficiency.

Carriers' fear of adverse selection among applicants in the small-group and individual markets motivates their behaviors. To avoid adverse selection, many carriers adopt selection mechanisms to screen out applicants who they suspect will use expensive medical care (Swartz and Garnick 1999, 2000a, b; Chollet and Kirk 1998). Such mechanisms include medical underwriting practices,[3] refusing to issue or renew a policy, red-lining certain industries and occupations, excluding coverage of services for pre-existing medical conditions, and differentiating their policies from their competitors' by generously covering some types of services (e.g., preventative) but limiting coverage of other services (e.g., substance abuse treatment) (Stone 1993; Frank *et al.* 1997).[4]

Thus, competition in insurance markets, especially the small-group and individual markets, focuses on how well carriers use mechanisms to identify which firms or individuals might be high risk versus low risk. As Newhouse pointed out in the context of risk adjustment models, a carrier only needs to be a little better than its competitors in the use of selection mechanisms to make more of a profit (Newhouse 1994). When carriers are not constrained in their ability to set different premiums for people who they believe have different probabilities of using expensive medical care, then carriers compete in large part in terms of the accuracy of their models for predicting a person's (or firm's) medical expenses. These models are generally known as actuarial models because they are based on actuarial tables of likelihoods of using different amounts of medical care by many different demographic and socioeconomic characteristics as well as health status and prior use of health care.[5] Different carriers will then price their health insurance policies to people and small firms based on the individual's or firm's expenditures predicted by each carrier's actuarial model. Usually, the models are used to determine how the premiums might be adjusted (underwritten) for particular individuals or firms. That is, if a small firm is predicted to have a high risk of high medical expenses in the next year because several people in the group had high expenses in the last year, the carrier may agree to offer insurance only if the firm pays a substantially higher amount over the basic premium for the policy.

While it might seem fair to charge higher premiums to insure people who have high probabilities of high medical expenses, this is true only if the models used to predict a person's risk of such expenses are accurate in their predictions. Unfortunately, they are not (Newhouse 1994). Nonetheless, carriers set very high premiums for people or small firms they do not want to cover because their models predict the people or firms have high risks of using expensive medical care. Some states permit carriers to deny an application for coverage without providing a reason. Where carriers cannot deny applications, they often can set premiums without significant constraints and they then use very high premiums to turn away would-be high-risk enrollees. Thus, very high premiums constitute an important barrier to coverage for people who are perceived by carriers' actuarial models to be high risk.

The actuarial models and underwriting principles also can cause carriers to exclude coverage for a medical condition to a group or person on the basis of information known by the carrier. Most states allow exclusion of coverage for a pre-existing condition (such as cancer, osteoarthritis, allergies) for a limited time period – typically twelve months. As a result, carriers more often simply deny an application if a person has had quite serious conditions, such as angina or a myocardial infarction (Chollet and Kirk 1998). In some states, underwriting of premiums is not permitted because it is viewed as a selection mechanism that discriminates against people if they are perceived to have high risks of expensive medical care. When underwriting is not permitted, or its use is restricted, carriers turn to other selection mechanisms to avoid insuring high-risk people.

A frequently used mechanism for separating high- and low-risk applicants consists of differentiating the benefits (or medical services) covered by a policy. If a carrier is able to identify a health care benefit that is particularly attractive to low-risk people but not to high-risk people, then it can design policies that cause people to voluntarily reveal that they are likely to be low- or high-risk people. Carriers' use of differences in benefits packages is a mechanism for getting individuals (or groups) to reveal information that is not available to carriers and that separates the individuals (or groups) in terms of risk levels for nominally unpredictable expensive medical events. Thus, for example, if a person knows that cancer runs in his or her family – which the carriers do not know – the person might choose a policy that has high upper limits on covered expenses, provides for cancer screening tests, and includes first-rate cancer centers in the list of providers. By choosing such a policy, the person is revealing information to the carrier regarding his or her risk expectations. Carriers have invested in substantial efforts to understand how differences in benefits packages can be used to attract low-risk people to some policies and high-risk people to other policies.

Carriers also have developed monopolistic market niches in the small-group and individual markets as another mechanism for avoiding adverse selection (Swartz and Garnick 2000a, b). In the individual markets, for example, some carriers specialize in marketing to individuals who have left the armed services; others specialize in policies attractive to very small firms of professionals (e.g., lawyers or financial advisors) or only to individuals who are self-employed. Many carriers also avoid insuring people in certain occupations or firms in specific industries – a practice often referred to as red-lining. For example, people who are hairdressers or florists often have difficulty obtaining health insurance because carriers expect a disproportionate share of such people to be at risk from HIV/AIDS. Similarly, people who are taxi drivers have a difficult time obtaining coverage because actuarial data indicate they frequently suffer from back troubles (due to long periods of sitting). Nonprofit small firms have problems finding insurers because such firms are thought to employ disproportionate numbers of people who have had physical or mental conditions. The result of this type of market niche specialization and avoidance of specific occupations or industries is that few carriers in a state market actively compete for business among all consumers seeking individual policies, and people whom insurers perceive as high risk have few, if any, options for obtaining health insurance (Pollitz *et al.* 2001; USGAO 1996).

The differences in states' regulations of the insurance markets within their borders permit the greater or lesser use of these mechanisms or different combinations of the strategies to avoid insuring high-risk people. States that have attempted to block carriers' use of such preferential selection mechanisms, particularly in the small-group or individual markets, have almost always set up regulations that block the use of only one or two of these mechanisms. State regulations, for example, might mandate that all policies sold in the state must cover substance abuse treatment so as to inhibit carriers' ability to avoid high-risk people who may want coverage of care for substance abuse. Some states have enacted regulations requiring carriers to accept any applicant ("guaranteed issue") so a carrier cannot turn down an applicant it views as high risk.[6] But of course, if a state has only one or two of these regulations in place, the carriers can use other mechanisms that are not proscribed to accomplish the same objective. For example, when a state requires carriers to accept any applicant but does not also have a regulation governing the way in which premiums can be set, we observe what should be a totally expected outcome: high-risk people are indeed offered coverage but at an extraordinarily high premium. Similarly, when states require community rating of premiums (say, in the small-group insurance market) but do not standardize the benefits to be covered in policies sold in the market, carriers can use differences in what benefits are covered under different policies to try to separate high-risk firms from low-risk firms.

In summation, the information asymmetries in health insurance markets – particularly the non-group and small-group markets – prevent the markets from being efficient. Enormous effort and expense are devoted to developing and applying selection mechanisms to avoid covering people who are likely to use expensive medical care. Carriers compete with each other not in terms of producing insurance *per se* at the lowest possible cost but in terms of insuring as high a proportion of low-risk people as possible in order to keep costs low. Thus, the usual competitive market forces that cause producers to seek profits by reducing their costs of production have been altered by the fear of adverse selection in non-group and small-group insurance markets. The competition among carriers consists of trying to do better than other carriers at selecting low-risk people, which involves efforts that do not contribute to producing insurance. The costs of creating and using selection mechanisms are a measure of the inefficiency that exists in health insurance markets.

How to address market failure: reduce fear of adverse selection

The regulatory efforts surrounding the non-group and small-group health insurance markets since 1990 generally did not focus specifically on carriers' fear of adverse selection. Instead, such efforts were targeted at eroding or blocking carriers' ability to use some of the selection mechanisms described earlier. The objective of these state regulations was to "level the playing field" of competition between carriers, especially in the non-group markets. By prohibiting some of the more obvious risk selection activities of carriers, policymakers hoped high-risk people would be spread randomly among the carriers so no one or two carriers would bear the burden of their costs. However, the initial or early generation of such regulatory efforts (dating from the late 1980s and early 1990s) consisted of just one or two regulations (such as requiring acceptance of all applicants, guaranteeing renewal of all policies, and restricting the length of time for excluding coverage of pre-existing conditions). In retrospect, it is not surprising that carriers responded to these efforts by using other selection mechanisms so as to avoid high-risk people.

New Jersey and New York, in what might be termed second-generation regulatory efforts with their non-group markets, invoked a set of regulations that were more sweeping in their ability to block carriers from pursuing selection mechanisms. New Jersey's Individual Health Coverage Program (IHCP), implemented in late 1993, consists of about eight regulations that effectively force the carriers to compete on the basis of premium rather than use selection mechanisms to attract or avoid applicants (Swartz and Garnick 2000a). Initially the IHCP was successful in terms of increasing the number of carriers competing in the market and achieving lower premiums. But a few small carriers lost money and then rapidly raised their rates in an attempt to sharply reduce the number of people they insured. The upshot was that people became confused by the rapid changes in premiums and left the market if they were relatively healthy, so premiums rose, further causing healthier people to leave the market (Monheit *et al.* 2004). New York's direct-pay (non-group) insurance market also has a sufficient number of regulations governing it so that all the HMOs in the state compete without the ability to select low-risk people. However, in New York there were large numbers of people with HIV/AIDS or other chronic conditions who were covered by the non-group market, so premiums were relatively high to begin with. As a result, few low-risk people have applied for coverage in the non-group market, and premiums have remained relatively high.

The bottom line is that the non-group markets are still riskier than the large-group market because they are voluntary and there is a very real potential for adverse selection in who chooses to apply for coverage. No amount of regulation aimed at leveling the playing field can get around that issue. Thus, if we want to increase access to health insurance markets for people without access to large-group insurance and reduce premiums – that is, if we want the markets to behave in a more traditionally competitive fashion – we need to reduce carriers' fear of adverse selection. This means that we need to reduce the risk to carriers that a few people will have extraordinarily high medical care costs and thereby drive carriers into bankruptcy.

Government as reinsurer: a proposal

To reduce this risk, state or federal governments could compensate carriers for most of the costs of extremely high-cost persons. For example, the government could pay a proportion of the costs of those individuals whose total annual medical costs exceed some threshold – say, $40,000 – or an amount that places a person's medical expenditures above the ninety-eighth or ninety-ninth percentile of the distribution of medical expenses of the entire population. Whether or not a person's medical care expenses would be eligible for reimbursement by the government would be determined after all the medical claims for a particular year had been filed (generally by March 31 of the year following a calendar year). That is, deciding whose expenses would be eligible for government reimbursement would be determined after the fact rather than based on a model of projected risk of high expenditures.

Carriers often purchase reinsurance to protect themselves from the risk that an insured's claims will exceed some amount. Reinsurance usually requires the original insurer (the carrier) to bear some portion of the costs above the threshold so the carrier will still have an incentive to continue to manage the health care of high-cost people. It would be important to retain this incentive if the government were to take on the role of reinsurer by reimbursing carriers for extremely high medical care expenses. The share of expenses that the government might cover also could vary over different "layers" of expenditures. For example, suppose the eligibility threshold were set at $40,000. The government could cover 90 percent of the costs from $40,000 to $75,000; then cover 85 percent of the costs between $75,001 and $150,000; then 90 percent of the costs between $150,001 and $500,000; and finally 95 percent of the costs above $500,000. Note that this reinsurance structure does not provide a limit to the losses that a carrier might face from an extremely high-cost person but it does significantly reduce the risk of extremely high losses faced by a carrier. An alternative structure of reinsurance layers could have the government cover 100 percent of the expenditures of someone above some level of spending (perhaps $500,000), and this would provide an upper limit to a carrier's potential losses per insured person.[7]

The cost of having the government take on the role of reinsurer in the non-group markets would depend on three factors: the threshold level of per-person expenditures at which the reinsurance would start, the percentages of carrier liability (the complement to the percent of expenses that the government would reinsure) in the successively higher layers of expenditures, and the benefits that would be included in the eligible set of benefits for reinsurance. Determining the threshold level at which government would take on the reinsurance responsibility will require analyses of medical care expenditures' data. We need to know what the costs are of people in the top 1 percent, top 2 percent, and top 3 percent of the expenditure distribution for people in the non-group and small-group markets. The Medical Expenditure Panel Survey (MEPS) is a good place to begin with estimating the total costs of people in each of these top percentile groups. However, even including people with large-group insurance coverage, the MEPS sample sizes are small for extensive analyses of the claims of people in the top few percentiles of the distribution. Large carriers' data on the medical expenditures of their enrollees may be needed to provide such estimates. With such data, simulations could be conducted to estimate the costs of a government reinsurance program in the non-group and/or small-group market – the simulations would vary the threshold levels at which the reinsurance would commence, as well as the shares of carrier liability in different layers of expenditures.

By having the government take responsibility for most of the expenses of people with extraordinarily high medical costs in a year – say for the people in the top 1 percent of the expenditure distribution of people with non-group and/or small-group coverage – the premiums for such coverage will be lower. The premiums will be lower because as much as 28 percent of the total expenditures are due to people in the top 1 percent of the distribution (Monheit 2003). With the government reinsuring these costs, carriers will not face the high risk they now face and they can lower their premiums. The government, acting as reinsurer, will shift the burden of the extremely high-cost insured people to the broad population base that pays taxes.

Without the reinsurance role of government, the burden of expenses for the extremely high-cost people covered by any one carrier would be borne by just the relatively small number of people who have non-group or small-group coverage from the carrier. As a result, the burden is felt as an increase in premiums by such people – and the increase is often significant enough that lower-risk individuals drop their coverage in response. If sufficient numbers of lower-risk people do this, it can set off a death spiral for the policy or carrier.

Thus, having the government provide reinsurance yields lower premiums both because it lowers the risk for the carriers and because it shifts the burden of the costs of extremely high-cost people to the broad population. The lower premiums provide a significant benefit to the goals of increasing the number of people with health insurance and creating more stable health insurance markets with lower premiums. The lower premiums will be attractive to low-risk people who want health insurance and currently choose not to purchase coverage because they think their expected medical costs are far less than premiums. With more low-risk people in the risk pool of people with non-group or small-group coverage, the premiums can remain low or even decline further.

There are at least two potential advantages to having the government act as reinsurer in these markets. One is that it is based on people's actual expenditures after the fact – it does not rely on prospective models of what a person's costs are likely to be. This is in direct contrast to programs that involve risk adjustments of premiums and high-risk pools. Risk adjustments and high-risk pools depend on models that estimate a person's likely medical expenses based on their characteristics and previous medical expenses or diagnoses. But these models are only predictive – and to date are relatively poor predictors of a person's predictable expenses. The second potential advantage of having the government act as reinsurer in these markets is that it could help restrain unnecessary expenditures. More attention will be focused on people whose care or diagnoses appear to be potentially very expensive. Often, people with extremely high medical care costs have had care that is not well managed, which contributes to the high costs (Lawrence 2003). It seems obvious that carriers should have a manager assigned to the care of people whose claims exceed some dollar amount or who have specific diagnoses. While some carriers have started to do this, many have not. If the government were the reinsurer in these markets, it could require carriers to institute management programs or face higher cost sharing by the carriers.

Lessons learned from past efforts: why government needs to focus on sources of market failure

As noted earlier, past reforms of the non-group and small-group insurance markets have not directly targeted the source of market failure in these markets. The rhetoric surrounding reform efforts usually implies that the reforms are intended to reduce the number of uninsured people or increase the number of people with small-group or non-group coverage. In many cases, the public also has been led to expect that the reforms will cause reductions in the premiums in these markets. Rarely do we find much discussion of the goal of stabilizing the market so the currently insured will be able to continue to have coverage, or discussion of an objective of increasing the number of carriers that sell policies in the market. Evaluations that have been done of some states' efforts have tended to focus simply on the numbers of people without health insurance and the premiums available in these markets. The evaluations generally have not analyzed what happened within the markets that might have caused observed changes in premiums and uninsured numbers. This is unfortunate, since it leaves us with little guidance as to how carriers reacted to various types of regulations. What then are we to make of states' efforts to use their regulatory powers to increase access to non-group and small-group insurance, and to stabilize these markets?

Two lessons emerge. One is that applying only one or two regulations to "level the playing field" of competition between carriers does not address the underlying source of market failure in the non-group and small-group markets. One or two regulations targeted at carriers' use of specific selection mechanisms do not cause high-risk people to be spread more randomly across carriers – carriers simply use other selection mechanisms to avoid covering people they perceive to be high risk. Applying a set of six or more regulations, which were designed as a package with the intent of blocking carriers' ability to use selection mechanisms, seems to achieve more premium competition and more accessibility to the markets. However, there is a tradeoff here for policymakers – if they effectively block carriers' ability to use selection mechanisms, they reduce choice and increase premiums for low-risk people. A full set of regulations to effectively block carriers' ability to use selection mechanisms includes standardizing the benefits packages that may be offered in the markets. Less choice of benefits packages increases the pooling of all risks in the market – which reduces premiums for high-risk people. Thus, the tradeoff is between the interests of low-risk and high-risk people. However, if the markets are not fully accessible by people perceived to be high risk, low-risk people eventually bear the burden of the costs of medical care obtained by high-risk people; such costs just occur outside the insurance markets.

The second lesson is that public policies are more successful in terms of achieving stability in premiums and carriers offering policies in the non-group and small-group markets when private policymakers are involved in designing the regulations. Private policymakers – primarily executives at carriers – know how carriers will respond to different types of regulations because they have first-hand knowledge of carriers' strategic thinking. They know how to frame a regulation so the incentives imbedded in the regulation create the desired response. In the cases of New Jersey's IHCP and New York's Healthy New York programs (Swartz 2001), the private policymakers were essential to focusing attention on the need for reducing the risk to carriers of adverse selection. Both programs' initial designs were constructed to shift the risk of extremely high costs from any one carrier to broader population bases – in New Jersey, to the insured population, and in New York, to the state's tax revenue base.

A further advantage of involving private policymakers in designing policies to stabilize markets is that when they are involved they have a stake in the outcome. Towards this end, state policymakers have potential leverage over the private policymakers in the form of their regulatory powers (Swartz and Garnick 1999). But unless the states (and the federal government) are willing to create a policy structure that provides relief from the risk of adverse selection, carriers have little reason to want to participate in market-based efforts to increase the number of people with private coverage.

Thus, in drawing lessons from prior regulatory efforts, it is important to evaluate the efforts in the context of what was occurring in the non-group or small-group market and not just whether the regulations reduced premiums or the number of uninsured. It may have been equally important that the regulations stabilized the market and achieved greater sharing of the burden of people with high medical care expenses. In thinking about future efforts to increase accessibility to the non-group and small-group markets for people without access to large-group insurance, policymakers need to focus on the root cause of market failure in these markets: the risk of adverse selection. The experiences of New Jersey and New York imply that private policymakers can contribute ideas towards how the burden of extremely high-cost people can be shared more broadly so the risk of adverse selection is greatly reduced. In both cases, the state's regulatory powers were used to set the conditions for competition in terms of premiums and to reduce the carriers' ability to use selection mechanisms.

Conclusions

Reducing the number of people without health insurance in the United States is a high priority for many policymakers. There is a strong preference among policymakers to reduce the number of uninsured by providing incentives for currently uninsured people to purchase coverage in the non-group and small-group insurance markets. One reason for this preference is that health insurance coverage is strongly rooted in the private market – two-thirds of the population has private health insurance coverage, primarily through employer-sponsored group coverage. Given the dynamic nature of health insurance coverage (Swartz *et al.* 1993; Nelson 2003), continuity of both health care and health insurance will be improved if more uninsured people have easy access to non-group and small-group markets.

Policymakers need to address the source of market failure in the non-group and small-group markets, however, if they expect to rely on private insurance markets to reduce the number of uninsured. Unless the carriers' risk of adverse selection is reduced in these markets, many uninsured people will not have access to the markets and premiums will be unaffordable. The carriers will use selection mechanisms to avoid covering high-risk people and premiums will remain high, reflecting the higher risk of insuring people in these markets.

Regulatory reforms of these markets may address carriers' fear of adverse selection if the regulations force carriers to compete in terms of premiums rather than their use of selection mechanisms. However, regulatory reforms generally do not directly address the carriers' fear of adverse selection and they have the potential for producing unintended consequences. In New Jersey, for example, the designers of the IHCP regulations did not anticipate that a number of small carriers would enter the market and cause significant losses (Swartz and Garnick 2000a). It was perfectly legal for these carriers to enter the market, but in hindsight, their participation in the IHCP caused havoc that destabilized the market.

A more direct method of reducing carriers' risk of adverse selection in the non-group and small-group markets is to have the government act as reinsurer for extremely high-cost people. Shifting the risk of extremely high costs from the carriers to a broader population base will reduce premiums, and enable the non-group and small-group markets to both operate more efficiently and be accessible to more people. Lower premiums ought to attract more low-risk people to the markets, thereby stabilizing them.

Notes

1 Of course, redistribution policies can create other inefficiencies – for example, people may alter their labor supply or other income-related activities so as to meet a program's income eligibility requirements.

2 Large employers have avoided state regulations and state taxes on health insurance by self-insuring (or self-financing) their employees' health care costs. The Employees Retirement and Income Security Act of 1974 (ERISA) exempts self-insured employers from state regulations and taxes on policies sold within a state. Most self-insured employers pay a fee to a third-party administrator (almost always a carrier) to administer the claims from medical care providers, and the employees are usually unaware that the third-party administrator is not their insurer as well.

3 Medical underwriting is the process by which carriers set the premium for an applicant based on the person's expected medical care costs. Thus, if a person has poor health status, actuarial underwriting practices would yield a higher premium than that for a similar person in excellent health. The underwriting process essentially determines whether a person pays an additional amount plus the base premium for the policy. Depending on state regulations, medical underwriting may be used by carriers writing policies for individuals, small groups, and particular individuals within small groups. The higher premiums that result from medical underwriting are also an effective method of screening out high-risk people, as I explain in the next section. High premiums discourage people from purchasing policies.

4 The Health Insurance Portability and Accountability Act of 1996 (HIPAA) has sometimes been mistakenly assumed to restrict these selection practices in the individual insurance market. HIPAA does not prohibit carriers from applying selection practices to the great majority of individuals who seek

coverage in the individual insurance markets. See Nichols and Blumberg (1998) for details.

5 Applicants in both the small-group and individual markets generally have to respond to questionnaires about their health status, use of medications and medical care in the past, and health risk behaviors. It is not unheard of for small groups to be offered coverage for most but not all of the members of the group – with the rejected members being denied coverage because carriers believe they will have high medical expenditures.

6 For example, Washington state's, New York's and New Jersey's individual insurance markets are required to guarantee issue of policies to any applicant regardless of the applicant's health status, age, gender, or place of residence.

7 In other contexts of bundled assets that are offered in secondary markets (for example, the secondary mortgage market), such layers are often referred to as "tranches." In reinsurance, the layers also imply differences in the level of liability for which the originating carrier is responsible.

References

Chollet, D.J. and Kirk, A.M. (1998) *Understanding Individual Health Insurance Markets: Structure, Practices, and Products in Ten States*. Menlo Park, CA: Henry J. Kaiser Family Foundation.

Chollet, D.J., Kirk, A.M., and Chow, M.E. (2000) *Mapping State Health Insurance Markets: Structure and Change in the States' Group and Individual Health Insurance Markets, 1995–1997*. Washington, DC: Academy for Health Services Research and Health Policy.

Frank, R.G., McGuire, T.G., Bae, J.P., and Rupp, A. (1997) "Solutions for Adverse Selection in Behavioral Health Care." *Health Care Financing Review*, 18 (3): 109–122.

Lawrence, D.M. (2003) "My Mother and the Medical Care Ad-hoc-racy." *Health Affairs*, 22 (2): 238–242.

Monheit, A.C. (2003) "Persistence in Health Expenditures in the Short Run: Prevalence and Consequences." *Medical Care*, 41 (7) supplement: 53–64.

Monheit, A.C., Cantor, J.C., Koller, M., and Fox, K.S. (2004) "Community Rating and Sustainable Individual Health Insurance Markets in New Jersey." *Health Affairs* 23 (4). In press.

Nelson, L. (2003) "How Many People Lack Health Insurance and for How Long?" Washington, DC: Congressional Budget Office. Online http://www.cbo.gov.

Newhouse, J.P. (1994) "Patients at Risk: Health Reforms and Risk Adjustment." *Health Affairs*, 13 (1): 132–146.

Nichols, L.M. and Blumberg, L.J. (1998) "A Different Kind of 'New Federalism'? The Health Insurance Portability and Accountability Act of 1996." *Health Affairs*, 17 (3): 25–42.

Pollitz, K., Sorian, R., and Thomas, K. (2001) *How Accessible is Individual Health Insurance for Consumers in Less-than-perfect Health?* Menlo Park, CA: Henry J. Kaiser Family Foundation.

Stone, D.A. (1993) "The Struggle for the Soul of Health Insurance." *Journal of Health Politics, Policy and Law*, 18 (2): 287–317.

Swartz, K. (2001) *Healthy New York: Making Insurance More Affordable for Low-income Workers*. Report 484, New York: Commonwealth Fund.

Swartz, K. and Garnick, D.W. (1999) "Can Adverse Selection be Avoided in a

Market for Individual Insurance?" *Medical Care Research and Review*, 56 (3): 373–388.

Swartz, K. and Garnick, D.W. (2000a) "Lessons from New Jersey's Creation of a Market for Individual Health Insurance." *Journal of Health Politics, Policy and Law*, 25 (1): 45–70.

Swartz, K. and Garnick, D.W. (2000b) "Adverse Selection and Price Sensitivity when Low-income People have Subsidies to Purchase Health Insurance in the Private Market." *Inquiry*, 37 (1): 45–60.

Swartz, K., Marcotte, J., and McBride, T.D. (1993) "Personal Characteristics and Spells without Health Insurance." *Inquiry*, 30 (1): 64–76.

US General Accounting Office (1996) *Private Health Insurance: Millions Relying on Individual Market Face Cost and Coverage Trade-offs*. GAO/HEHS-97–8.

12 Conclusions

Alan C. Monheit and Joel C. Cantor

The chapters of this volume have provided a comprehensive review of empirical research findings, applied methodologies, and policy implications and alternatives associated with the regulation of health insurance in the small-group and individual insurance markets. Given the breadth of the discussion presented, we now provide a summing up of a number of salient points provided by our contributors. Among the key conclusions reached by the contributors are the following:

- Reform of the small-group insurance market has not resulted in market chaos. Research generally finds that reform has had little impact on coverage or uninsured rates. However, more stringent reforms may have yielded gains in coverage for high-risk employees of small firms relative to lower-risk employees.
- There has been surprising little research on the impact of small-group market reform on employment-based health insurance premiums and on secondary labor market outcomes such as employment, hours worked, and employee wages.
- There are relatively few empirical studies of reform's impact on coverage rates and premiums in the individual insurance market. Empirical findings regarding the impact of reform on coverage rates and market structure tend to be mixed and inconsistent. As with small-group reform, there is some evidence that more stringent rating reform may have reduced coverage rates for healthier adults relative to higher-risk adults.
- The small size of the individual insurance market, its potential volatility due to short-term enrollment and relatively high premiums, and the market's sensitivity to economic conditions cast doubt on whether reform in this market can successfully achieve its coverage goals.
- Efforts to empirically identify and obtain unbiased estimates of a causal relationship between health insurance market reform and outcomes of interest confront a number of significant methodological challenges. These include the selection of pre- and post-reform observation periods; appropriate choice of treatment and control groups;

adequate sample size for treatment groups; potential policy endogeneity; adequacy of data to characterize individual risk profiles; and key assumptions that the characteristics of treatment and control groups remain constant over time and that control groups are unaffected by reform.

- Reform relies on voluntary responses by potential enrollees to achieve expanded coverage. Consequently, demand-side factors and coverage affordability may be more important in expanding health insurance coverage than the supply-side constraints addressed by insurance market reform.
- Political realities regarding reform implementation, tradeoffs that determine winners and losers, contentious and exaggerated claims regarding reform, and rising health insurance premiums pose significant impediments to the effectiveness of reform.
- Reform has not adequately addressed the adverse selection concerns of health insurance carriers.
- With its current policy tools, reform is unlikely to achieve the goals of expanded coverage and stability of premiums, market enrollment and insurer participation. Supplementing existing reform provisions with risk-adjusted payments to insurers and use of high-risk pools may help to allay carrier fears of adverse selection. Alternative approaches to reform, such as risk-based subsidies to high-risk and low-income enrollees and retrospective carrier reinsurance can, in theory, address equity and efficiency issues. This is necessary to ensure adequate enrollment and insurer participation.

As noted, the balance of the research findings suggest that reform in both the small-group and individual markets has not been successful in achieving expanded health insurance coverage and may, in fact, have resulted in some unintended consequences for low-risk individuals. This raises the compelling question of why reform has not met expectations. Here the contributors offer several explanations. Kosali Simon and Deborah Chollet note that expectations as to what reform could realistically achieve may have been overstated. Thomas Buchmueller also remains skeptical about the ability of reform to meet expectations. He notes that the insurer practices that motivated reform may not have been a major reason for the low rates of insurance provision by small firms and that, even if so, reform may not have substantially altered insurer practices Buchmueller speculates that the ability of reform to increase coverage by addressing insurer underwriting practices may have been limited to perhaps just a small number of very high-risk consumers.

Perhaps most prominently, reform has focused almost exclusively on supply-side practices, placing great faith in voluntary responses by employees, employers, and individuals to the access and rating provisions used to encourage coverage expansions. As Thomas Buchmueller, Sanford

Herman, and Susan Marquis have noted, it may have been unrealistic to expect a high degree of demand-side responsiveness to reform. This is especially the case when much of the period of reform implementation (the late 1980s to mid-1990s) was confronted by rising premiums and stagnant employee income. Next, as Susan Marquis and Katherine Swartz have emphasized, reform has done little to allay insurer concerns regarding adverse selection. Thus, while reform sought to address the most explicit insurer selection practices, more subtle practices regarding health plan benefits (e.g., inclusion of benefits of dubious value and exclusion of benefits more valuable to high risks) and premium setting (taking advantage of allowable flexibility in rating restrictions) may have discouraged enrollment.[1]

Other factors impeding reform's performance also warrant consideration. The political and market environments confronting reform may have also contributed to its lack of success through pressures for cost-enhancing benefit expansions (Steven Larsen), contentious and inaccurate claims regarding reform's performance (Karen Pollitz), and in the case of the individual market reform, a highly concentrated market insulated from possible favorable competitive effects of reform (Deborah Chollet). As Len Nichols notes, the complexity of insurance contracts and the institutional realities of regulatory compliance also raise questions about the effectiveness of efforts to enforce reform. Nichols observes that one cannot be completely confident that an actuary's certification of carrier compliance will achieve *actual* compliance. Moreover, he notes that enforcement of reform is generally passive, based upon complaints by market participants (such as agents and brokers) with little incentive to engage in actions that would trigger enforcement efforts. Finally, one can only speculate whether state governments and their departments of insurance have the resources to vigorously review carrier responses to a new and possibly complex set of insurance market regulations.

In assessing the research findings, we must also be mindful of the importance of the methodological challenges and data requirements confronting researchers. Given the strong public interest in expanding health insurance coverage and the lack of a strong consensus on how to proceed, an evaluation of state initiatives that address a key part of the coverage equation – insurance market imperfections and insurer behavior – was certainly warranted. Moreover, as Barbara Schone has observed, economic theory provides little guidance regarding expected outcomes from reform implementation. Thus, the empirical work summarized in this volume provides an essential first assessment of what can be gleaned from efforts to apply conventional survey data and a variety of empirical approaches to examine the impact of alternative reform regimes. However, as Thomas Buchmueller and Barbara Schone have described, the requirements for such research are daunting.

Having said this, it is our hope that this volume will encourage future researchers to take up the challenge of improving on the first- and second-generation studies of reform, fill in gaps in the research regarding the individual insurance market and the behavior of health insurance premiums, explore the longer-term consequences of reform, and examine other outcomes of reform and secondary effects on the labor market that have not or have only minimally been considered by existing studies. Such research, together with work on the political economy and institutional facets of reform, will improve our understanding of the costs and benefits of reform implementation. Finally, it is our hope as well that the policy implications developed by the contributors to this volume will contribute to the debate on how best to re-structure reform to make it a more effective policy tool in expanding health insurance coverage.

Note

1 See Hall (2000/2001) for a discussion of how insurers may use allowable flexibility in rating provisions to risk select in the small-group market.

Reference

Hall, M.A. (2000/2001) "The Structure and Enforcement of Health Insurance Rating Reforms." *Inquiry*, 37: 376–388.

Index

A page number followed by an "f" indicates a figure; a page number followed by a "t" indicates a reference to a table; a page number followed by an "n" indicates a reference to a footnote.